The Nitpicker's Guide to the Movies

Volume 2

By

Will Nuessle

The Nitpicker's Guide to the Movies

Volume 2

Copyright © 2011 by William Nuessle

No part of this book may be reproduced or transmitted in any form or by any means, graphic, electronic, or mechanical, including photocopying, recording, taping, or by any information storage retrieval system, without the written permission of the author.

You should take the above seriously, as he is a ninja.

Table of Contents

Foreword

Foreword

By the Numbers!!! (Volumes 1-5, that is)

Total movies reviewed: 50

Total movies with Will Smith in a lead role: 4

Orlando Bloom: 5

Tom Cruise: 1 (thankfully)

Daniel Radcliffe, Emma Watson, Rupert Grint: 6

Total movies James Cameron had his hands all over: 3, including the top 2, Avatar and Titanic

Peter Jackson: 4 (All three Lord of the Rings movies, King Kong)

Steven Spielberg: 7 (Back to the Future, Men In Black, Raiders, E.T., The Lost World, Jurassic Park, War of the Worlds) [See Volume 3 for why my Top 50 list is different than current Official Top 50 Lists]

George Lucas: 7 (All six <u>Star Wars</u> movies, of course, but he was also Executive Producer on <u>Raiders</u>)

John Williams: 17 (it's good to be the king!)

Total movies made in the 1970s: 1 (<u>Star Wars IV</u>)

The 1980s: 6 (<u>Back to the Future</u>, <u>Ghostbusters</u>, <u>E.T.</u>, <u>Star Wars V</u>, <u>Star Wars VI</u>, <u>Raiders</u>)

The 1990s: 9 (<u>Armageddon</u>, <u>Men in Black</u>, <u>Jurassic Park</u>, <u>The Lost World</u>, <u>Star Wars I</u>, <u>Toy Story</u>, <u>Independence Day</u>, <u>Terminator II</u>, <u>Titanic</u>)

The last ten years: 34 (and they've all been sooooo great!)

Total animated movies: 9 (<u>Toy Story</u>, <u>Kung Fu Panda</u>, <u>The Incredibles</u>, <u>Ice Age 2</u>, <u>Ice Age 3</u>, <u>Ratatouille</u>, <u>Toy Story 3</u>, <u>Finding Nemo</u>, <u>Shrek 2</u>)

Total movies featuring superheroes or magical powers: 29 (we do like escapism, don't we?)

Total movies with some form of giant creature (if it's gigantic to our heroes, i.e. the shark in <u>Finding Nemo</u>, that counts): 33 (which surprised me)

Total movies involving time travel: 3 (<u>Back to the Future</u>, <u>Terminator II</u>, <u>Harry Potter and the Prisoner of Azkaban</u>)

Total movies where the concept came from a book (or comic book, or it's a sequel to a movie that came from a book): 21 (and the book is <u>always</u> better!)

Total movies based on something that actually happened: 1 (<u>Titanic</u>)

Total movies featuring aliens or extraterrestrial life: 11

Total independent films: 0

Total chick-flicks: 0

Total comedies: 0

Total documentaries: 0

Schizophrenic Series Award: <u>Harry Potter</u> (six movies, two different Dumbledores, four different directors!)

Nice Try But No Dice Award: George Lucas (Star Wars 4-6 wondrous!   Star Wars 1-3 putrid!)

Character Seen Most: It's a tie between R2-D2, C3PO, Ben Kenobi and Harry Potter, Hermione Granger, Ron Weasley and company with 6 appearances apiece

Total words in Nitpickers Guide Volumes 1-5: 200,000, give-or-take

Total hours spent creating Nitpickers Guide Volumes 1-5: 250 and counting

Was It Worth It: yes, and thanks for coming along with me!

<u>If</u> this is your first NGM experience, welcome aboard--and if you like Volume 2, you'll love 3-5!

Enough with the foreword...<u>forward</u>!

#11:   **Harry Potter and the Half-Blood Prince**

Ruminations: final Potter film!   Out of all umpteen!

-0:00:42 Harry is having to deal with his godfather, the only family he had left, having just been murdered. Can't Dumbledore do <u>something</u> to shield Harry from the magical press?

-0:01:45 Is it just coincidence that the cloud looks like a skull?   Of course not.   So right after his big defeat by Dumbledore, as he runs of in disgrace, Voldy still has power to burn, making things out of clouds up where nobody can see?

-0:02:10 What is this form of travel the Deatheaters are using?   It's not a broomstick, they're not apparating...it's cool but never explained

-0:02:45 How are these Deatheaters wrecking the bridge?

-0:03:03 Standard question: where'd they get that high-up-in-the-air picture of the bridge devastation?

-0:03:20 If Harry's reading a magical paper around Muggles, how does he keep the pictures from moving, giving himself away?

-0:03:40 Continuity, newspaper!   It was off the edge of the table a frame ago--not anymore

-0:03:49 Continuity--newspaper went back over the edge again

-0:04:24 Hey, Dumbledore's on the platform!   What caused Harry to start looking over here in the first place, tho?

-0:06:40 Interesting that the blood only starts dripping as Harry looks at the paper.   There's no spots there before--nicely timed arrival, apparently!

-0:06:49 ...and then it <u>stops</u> dripping right away. Weird

-0:07:00 The man-out-of-armchair bit is just tremendous!   This series has truly wonderful special effects--and unlike the <u>Star Wars</u> prequel, I kinda care about what happens to the main characters

-0:08:28 That repair-everything-in-sight spell sure must come in handy.   I admit I'm jealous

-0:08:45 "Mind if I use the loo?"   Why would he mind?   It ain't his house

-0:09:37 For someone who is constantly on the run, that's a lot of pictures to have on the end-table

-0:10:38 "Horace, you mind if I take this?"   Once again, Dumbledore--this isn't Horace's house!

-0:10:50 If they're just passing through, why'd Dumbledore fix everything?   Horace will have to put it back into disrepair now

-0:12:20 Was it a little joke of Dumbledore's, to apparate Harry into the stream like that?

-0:12:38 Well, when'd Ginny get all purty and stuff?

-0:14:12 So it's okay to do magic outside Hogwarts now?   Since when?

-0:18:03 We're really letting Bellatrix the half-insane dictate the terms of the Unbreakable Vow?   Sheesh

-0:18:30 The spell thread disappears.   Who told it to go?   How'd it know Bella was finished?

-0:19:45 I just love the Weasley brothers, and wish I could take a turn through their shop

-0:21:25 Lucky Draco didn't look around, as Harry and Ron are <u>clearly</u> in his line of sight

-0:23:07 Sixth movie and we finally see something of the life on the Hogwarts Express! About time

-0:23:53 Continuity as Harry leaves the carriage

-0:25:57 Pulling the shade in the window causes all the shades in the car to go? That's convenient. And what's with the big Slytherin car when the Gryffindors are cramped into individual compartments? Why aren't they all the same?

-0:26:13 How'd Draco know about the invisibility cloak?

-0:26:31 I think I'll give this the Will Award--how lucky is Harry that (a) Draco doesn't steal the extremely rare and expensive invisibility cloak and how even more lucky is Harry that Draco doesn't (b) <u>kill him</u>? Or at least seriously injure him? The kick in the face is harsh, but hardly debilitating

-0:27:10 Sure is lucky Luna came along, also--when even Ron and Hermione weren't looking for Harry!

-0:28:00 They're so serious about Hogwarts security--yet they only ask Harry and Luna's <u>names</u>? How is that proof against polyjuice potionery?

-0:28:55 Harry's gonna let Luna perform emergency magical surgery? That kick to the head must've knocked something loose

-0:29:54 We haven't seen the Sorting Hat much since the second movie. That makes me sad

-0:30:02 Huh, the magical effect with the owl at Dumbledore's podium--that's a first!

-0:30:47 Those tubes at the right, are those for the House Cup award? Something <u>else</u> we haven't seen since the first movie...the books are so much better!!

-0:33:08 Ron:"I don't want to take potions. Quidditch trials coming up, I need to practice!" Yeah, I forgot--Ron's on the Quidditch team now. They left out everything in the last two movies, didn't they?

-0:34:20 Hermione is attracted to freshly mown grass? I admit it's a pleasant smell, but...girl needs to get out more

-0:35:01 Whoa, major continuity! Slughorn has the Felix Felisis potion at roughly chest level, then the shot changes and he's holding it high in the air!

-0:35:35 "--to the student who manages to brew an acceptable draft of Living Death." So it's that hard, that he doesn't think any of them can do it?   What if two manage? (Never mind, only Potter'll do it anyway)

-0:37:00 So Snape's old potions book is just lying around?   Seems like that's something he would have wanted to hide away

-0:41:10 Riddle must be really hard up for company, to tell secrets to this stranger--what do people normally do to him when they hear he can "move objects without touching them"?

-0:43:15 Continuity, Harry's face as shot changes

-0:43:50 Is there a point to the cage-in-a-cage besides looking interesting?

-0:45:03 The Gryffindor team was mostly knocking about, then Ginny yells "Shut it!" and less than a second later they're all in line!   Amazing!

-0:46:24 Amazed they play the dangerous game of Quidditch without helmets

-0:46:48 "Come on, Ron."   Harry seems perturbed-- Ron's a moment away from a fifty foot fall, he's hanging off his broom, and Harry's just annoyed with him?

-0:49:40 Harry says "Don't sit beside me," indicating the seat across from him.   Huh?   That some English turn of phrase we don't get here across the pond?

-0:51:38 The desperate thing Hermione has for Ron in this movie is painful to watch

.

-0:51:50 Ron whispering to Harry when he's only about a foot behind Hermione--why does he think she can't hear him?

-0:52:07 And of course Harry's <u>right there</u> for an important, unexplained magical happening

-0:54:42 Alan Rickman is sooooo good as Snape

-0:54:50 The Marauder's map seems to have changed graphical form--but then it's magic, so I suppose it can do that

-0:56:35 Continuity, ice cream (and it was inevitable)

-0:56:55 Where did these new twins come from? I'm sure students would escape my notice, but twins?

-0:57:09 Is there a reason why neither Harry nor Hermione are eating?   That ice cream looks pretty good

-0:58:20 Slughorn's hourglass: "The sand runs in accordance with the quality of the conversation."   That's pretty subjective magical sand there

-0:58:50 "Did Voldemort ever make the shelf, sir?" Wow, gets right to the point, doesn't he?   Could at least say "Tom Riddle" and soften the blow a bit

-1:01:30 It's weird that it turns out later Harry <u>didn't</u> put the Liquid Luck into Ron's cup--because it suuuure looks like he did, there was a flash and everything!

-1:01:56 As well as no helmets, there's no eye protection?   I wonder how these Quidditch competitors can see anything

-1:02:01 The snow on the lens is a nice touch, as this whole scene is done digitally

-1:02:15 There's no evidence of Luna's crazy hat letting out roars--which it did in the book...

-1:03:00 Since she still thinks he's cheating, I'm surprised at how happy Hermione looks at Ron's success. Then again, young love...

-1:09:13 No.   Neville's <u>serving</u> at Slughorn's party? Booo!

-1:11:40 Why did Draco try to crash Slughorn's party?   What possible reason would he have for wanting to be here?

-1:12:27 ...and how'd Potter get waaay down the corridor, to a hiding place, before Snape and Malfoy came out of the room?

-1:14:45 Continuity, Harry's head

-1:16:54 The Order (the good guys) knows that Malfoy was investigating a Vanishing Cabinet, a device that can transport people anywhere, and they just <u>leave it</u>? That'll be a bummer later, I betcha...

-1:18:28 These two trained Order of the Phoenix types can't get through the fire, and fifth-year Ginny <u>can</u>?

-1:20:15 Figure Harry is once again lucky to be alive, as he has once again walked right into a trap.   Chosen One maybe, but Stupid One also

-1:23:30 Interesting that the point-of-view of a person's memory would be outside the person's own head, hmmm?

-1:26:00 "Is that what you told Tom Riddle when he came asking questions?"   Master of subtlety, this one

-1:27:50 I wonder who Romilda got to deliver the sweets to Harry's bedside--since females aren't able to get into male dormitories and vice versa

-1:29:32 Continuity, the level in Ron's glass.   He only took one sip, and then next shot it's half empty

-1:29:50 Slughorn is giving underage students liquor? Seriously?

-1:30:27 Does CPR not work on magical folks?

-1:30:53 Once again Harry is right in the middle of a magical mishap

-1:33:10 It was a lucky, lucky thing Harry got that Potions book--without it he wouldn't have won the Liquid Luck that he needs, Ron would be dead...

-1:33:44 Once again Harry skulks after Draco who doesn't see him, though Potter is in plain sight

-1:34:12 Draco yanks the rug off the Vanishing Cabinet for what seems like the twelfth time--why does he keep covering it?   Don't others know it's here?

-1:34:34 How come Draco didn't have to say the magic words this time?

-1:35:00 Draco already proved this thing worked with the apple--why the second test?

-1:38:39 I don't know how any order is kept at all in a school where the students have magical wands, and can just throw hexes at each other

-1:38:50 Harry's been around the magical community for six years now.   There is <u>no</u> excuse for him using a spell when he didn't even know what it would do. He really deserves expulsion this time

-1:40:33 What are the odds!   Ginny, Ron's baby sister and the girl Harry likes, knows of a room where you can put things to get rid of them!   The same room Draco's been going to!

-1:42:07 Going to all this trouble to hide the book-- it's a book!   You've got a wand--<u>burn</u> it!

-1:43:00 So now we've seen a Vanishing Cabinet in Diagon Alley, and we've seen a Vanishing Cabinet at Hogwarts, in an area Malfoy's been skulking around.   Hmm, Harry, maybe you should <u>tell somebody about it</u>!

But of course he doesn't

-1:43:04 I've crabbed in other reviews about how Malfoy never seemed to get in serious trouble--now I'm agog that Harry isn't packing his bags

-1:45:24 Now that Slughorn isn't leaning in the window, those moving plants have curiously stopped moving

-1:45:58 When did these students start wearing regular clothes instead of robes all the time?

-1:46:06 Really, really, really coulda done without the gigantic dead spider

-1:46:42 As well as making you lucky, the Felix Felisis apparently also makes a person sort-of drunk

-1:47:44 I'm very thankful Aragog's family is not at the burial

-1:53:15 "This is very dark stuff, Tom, very dark indeed."   And it's available in a school library, even the restricted section, because...

-1:53:53 So, Hor Cruxes.   One splits one's soul and puts a piece into an object, and if one is then killed, one lives on in that object.

Doesn't sound like much of a life, frankly

-1:57:30 Dumbledore, to Harry: "You need a shave, my friend."   Look who's talking

-1:57:50 "You still look the same to me, sir." Obviously Harry has no memory of what Dumbledore looked like his first two years (wink, wink)

-1:58:13 There isn't a better person Dumbledore could take?   McGonagle, Mad-Eye Moody, Arthur Weasley, anybody?   Of course there is, but it's Harry's story so if he doesn't go, neither do we.   But still...

-1:58:29 "Should I tell you to abandon me and save yourself, you must do so."   Um...how?   Kid can't apparate, can he?

-2:00:22 Okay, so blood had to be spilled to gain access to the hidden cave.   Does it make sense for Dumbledore to cut right across his palm?   Couldn't he do a fingertip, an earlobe, something not so vital?

-2:01:15 Use the Force, Dumbledore...

-2:02:36 "It has to be drunk.   All of it."   A, how does he know, and 2, why?   Can't you just spill the stuff on the ground?

-2:03:00 "It's your job to make sure I keep drinking this potion, Harry, even if you have to force it down my throat."   How, exactly, does one force another to drink something that person does not wish to?

-2:05:55 Harry can't figure out a way to get water from the basin to Dumbledore's mouth?   He's got his cupped hands, he's got a shirt on--kid ain't very clever   (it wouldn't be very dignified, but the big D is dying)

-2:07:21 Well, these things sure are nasty

-2:08:23 I'm not sure why they have to get back in the boat, and can't just apparate out of the cavern

-2:15:00 I'm not sure why the Deatheaters are traipsing through the forest, and not back into the Vanishing Cabinet from whence they came

-2:16:33 The Dark Mark seems changed from movie 4--gotta stay up-to-date, that Voldemort

-2:19:54 Who put Dumbledore's wand back here? Especially considering how very important it is?

-2:21:33 Wow, that was a long message to write on a tiny scrap of paper.   Guy must've had seriously good handwriting

#12:   Star Wars I: The Phantom Menace

Ruminations: There already is a nitpicking book out about the Star Wars series, written by T.A. Chapin and Polly Luttrell.   They've collectively seen these movies hundreds of times, and you'd think their book would be definitive.   HA! In this movie alone, I found over 25 they missed--lots of continuity errors.   And it was nice to have something to make me happy, as this movie is annoying and I don't like it. And awaaay we go!

-0:02:02 Just how many ships does it take, to block access to an entire planet?   Or is the important stuff on Naboo all on one side?   (It's just there's a whole lot of space out there, is all)

-0:03:00 The droid that meets our Jedi heroes looks almost exactly like Threepio!   Except for being a different color!   Has a similarly prissy voice, too!   What are the odds...

-0:03:30 Is there some Force-related reason why Jedi Padawans have to have really stupid hairdos?

-0:03:50 I certainly don't mind, but it's interesting that the Trade Federation non-humans talk to each other in English

-0:04:10 Nice shot of the crew in shiny Threepi--um, I mean droid TC-14

-0:06:22 That Kenobi, always trying to impress his master. Three seconds ago he deflected a droid blaster shot back to its originator, who fell to the floor. Wide shot shows all droids dealt with. Cut to Master Qui-Gon, then back to Kenobi...who is suddenly decapitating another droid! Which he must have quickly picked up off the floor just so he could get another hit in and look good!

-0:06:42 Qui-Gon is sure tough. Now that the bridge's blast doors are closed, his lightsaber half-circle cut won't do, so he shoves the blade right into the doors. His hands are inches from the molten metal he was just cutting, but he apparently feels no pain!

-0:07:03 The droidekas are <u>really</u> cool. Too bad they're in no more than a minute of this way-too-long movie

-0:09:24 "A communications disruption can mean only one thing: invasion." They must have <u>really</u> good communications--here on Earth, communications disruptions can come due to sunspots, hurricanes, guys from the sewer company cutting the lines...

-0:10:00 I swear I'll only say it once per <u>Star Wars</u> movie: sure is <u>loud</u> in space

-0:10:30 Why does a droid need to look at a hologram? Why can't the Trade Fed yahoos just talk to him over radio?

-0:11:00 And the introduction of everybody's favorite character, Jar-Jar the Ridiculous Stereotype! Sure wish he'd been in the classic films, don't we?

-0:11:06 Lucky the ship going <u>over</u> Qui-Gon and Jar-Jar doesn't do them any damage--repulsorlifts and all, but they're fine! Wow!

-0:11:53 "You saved my again." At least Jar-Jar is fulfilling the character-who-doesn't-speak-English-well requirement. Since Yoda isn't in this movie much

By the way, on the commentary right about now Lucas starts talking about how he loves this scene, because it was the first time a truly digital character had interacted with real humans in the SW universe. And all I can think of is, "Yeah, Jar-Jar looks pretty real, too bad I <u>hate</u> him!!!" I don't care how real it looks, if I don't <u>care</u> you've missed the point, George!

-0:13:13 How convenient! Previously unheard-of underwater breathing apparatus-es! Just what they needed! Hope they last long enough to get the boys to the underwater city...

-0:14:04 I have trouble believing the bubble they just walk through without letting any water in or air out

-0:15:47 Again with the Jedi mind-trick. Is Qui-Gon putting the whammy on everybody? If not, why does no-one protest or question Boss Nass' decisions? (I guess nobody questions the Boss)

-0:15:56 Is Nass yanking the Jedi's collective chains? "The quickest way to reach the Naboo is through the planet's <u>core</u>?" Even if there was a way to get to Japan from Tucson via the center of the Earth, I still can't imagine how it would be faster (what with molten stuff, you know?) Plus, the Jedi ran from the Trade Federation ships, swam down here, and now it turns out all the Naboo are on the other side of the <u>planet</u>? That seems totally wrong--kinda like these movies

-0:16:39 "He owes me what you call a 'life-debt'." Suppose this isn't a nit, but I thought life-debts were just a Wookiee thing

-0:17:18 Again with air-to-water transfer through bubble, no air lost or water in.   This time it's done with a fast-mover...but I still don't buy it being that perfect

-0:17:30 The sub is pretty cool.   Sure is lucky Jar-Jar can help navigate

-0:18:03 I pity the subtitler having to deal with Jar-Jar's horrible attempts at English.   But I question writing up the word "accident-es" as "axadentes"

-0:19:00 Boy, this Trade Federation stuff sure makes for an excitin' movie, don't it?   Much better than seeing Jedis train, or fight, or <u>anything</u>...

-0:20:46 Let's remember the Trade Federation droids have to go around the whole planet, apparently, to get to the Naboo.   While our Jedi friends are going through the <u>core</u>, because that makes sense.   So here we see Trade Federation ships slowly advancing on the Naboo-ians.   How long did that take?   These things move about 30 miles an hour, and they had to circumnavigate the globe!

-0:21:18 "Viceroy, we have captured the queen." Yeah, Lucas, don't <u>show</u> us this stuff, that might be actually interesting.   Just tell us.   We'll still be happy, 'cause it's the SW universe and anything you do is wonderful...

-0:21:24 Whoa! The journey through the planet core comes to an end in a nice, Venice-like fishing pond! What fun!

-0:21:10 So did Queen Amidala change from the stupid, red, lantern-bearing dress into this stupid, black, how-many-ravens-died-to-make-that-thing dress after she was captured? Nice of the droids to let her have wardrobe access

-0:21:52 Continuity, bottom of the stairs

-0:22:00 Huh, what a coincidence. The droid answers a command by saying "Roger," almost as if it had been on Earth at some point

-0:22:48 I guess this isn't a nit--but if I were Qui-Gon, I wouldn't be so casual about flipping a lightsaber I just deactivated into my cloak. You slip on the button and that'd be one heck of a wound

-0:23:10 Continuity, Qui-Gon hair (one of many)

-0:24:50 Some battle-hardened pilots these guys are...surrounded by loser droids, they let Obi-Wan do all the fighting, and just sit on their cans until all the droids are downed

-0:26:05 "The shield generator's been hit!" Well, why is it on the outside of the ship, you morons?

-0:26:10 Considering all the laser fire they've been taking, and how long the shield generator is down or at least damaged, sure is lucky everybody but droids we didn't care about survived.

-0:26:11 "We'll be sitting ducks."   Amazing that the phrase "sitting ducks" was in use a long time ago in a galaxy far, far away!

-0:27:40 Nice feature on the hologram, the Drama setting...Sidious is talking to the Trade Fed yahoos, and suddenly Darth Maul just saunters into the hologram.   I'm not sure how they <u>did</u> that, what hologram setting allows for that, but it sure looked cool, didn't it?

-0:28:10 Okay, here's another example of why these prequel movies suck.   Maybe it was important to have Artoo save the ship, to introduce this droid we'll see again and again--and I like Artoo, don't get me wrong.   But now they're introducing the droid to the Queen?   That's like presenting a medal to the hyperdrive computer!   Who cares what the droid thinks, especially Queen Dipsy-Doodle?

-0:28:20 continuity, Artoo's light as shot changes

-0:28:35 Amidala tells Padme, who is really the real queen (right?   That got ever so slightly confusing) to clean up Artoo.   Either the queen's double just told the queen to do some grunt work, or the queen just told her double to do grunt work, but either way, a <u>really</u> important person was just tasked with a menial job for <u>no reason!</u>

Except that Padme has to meet Jar-Jar somehow, I suppose, and since they couldn't get a <u>good</u> writer for this movie...

-0:29:13 Continuity, Jar-Jar's hands. Considering this character is <u>completely digital</u>, there is no excuse for a continuity error!

-0:30:10 "Don't let them send any transmissions." Qui-Gon, to Obi-Wan. Does Kenobi really have the right to restrict Naboo communications like that?

-0:30:50 Why is Artoo going along, on the Tatooine excursion? Did he do such a great job on the blockade escape that he's earned shore leave?

-0:31:30 Seems odd that Qui-Gon and Padme would leave Artoo so far behind. Coupla guys come along and snatch him pretty easy, I figure

-0:32:24 Once again, as so often happens, one of the main characters goes up a flight of stairs with no thought for poor Artoo the rolling droid...

-0:32:34 Whaddya know--they have <u>angels</u> in this long ago, far far away galaxy

-0:32:55 Look at cute little Anakin Skywalker, before he got all whiny and Darksidey and annoying...

-0:34:17 Continuity, Watto.   He goes from just above Qui-Gon's eye level to just below from one frame to the next...

-0:35:42 Whaddya know--twirling a finger by one's ear is the sign for "crazy" in this long ago, far far away galaxy

-0:36:08 The snack treat that Jar-Jar sends flying at Sebulba flies awful slowly

-0:36:15 Did Sebulba bounce?   Shot before this he was heading down, cut shot and he's heading down again. Then a slight continuity glitch as Jar-Jar falls backwards.

-0:36:50 I don't know much about slavery--thank goodness--but if I did own a slave, letting him wander freely through a marketplace would seem foolish.   What if somebody took Anakin for themselves?   They could even get him off-planet if they wanted

-0:38:45 Forget about how ridiculous it is that a slave can get parts for a robot, much less one as complicated as Threepio--is that a jai alai paddle hanging from the wall in the back of the shot?   Did Anakin used to play the game before he got into podracing?

-0:39:00 "Where is everybody?"   Threepio has one photoreceptor on--can't he sort-of see?

And why would Annie's mom need a protocol droid fluent in over six million forms of communication anyway? Kid oughta build them a Tatooine escape pod

-0:39:38 Why does the <u>robot</u> care that his parts are showing?   Why did Anakin build him with the Prissiness module?

-0:41:01 Continuity as Anakin says "boom!"   Right before Jar-Jar utters his hilarious trademark phrase "How wude!"

-0:43:14 Momma needs to make up her mind.   She just said that Watto won't let Anakin race, and now she says that she dies every time Watto <u>makes</u> him race.   Which is it?

-0:44:43 "My ship will be the entry fee."   A--that ship isn't his anymore than Artoo was earlier, where does Qui-Gon get off claiming everything in sight?   B--where'd he get that cool mini-hologram model of the Queen's vessel?

-0:47:20 "There was no father."   Hey, since George can't come up with any good ideas of his own, he might as well borrow from the Bible!   Problem is, the story of Jesus is true, the virgin birth, all of it--and I do not appreciate a crappy sci-fi trilogy glomming onto it for perceived legitimacy

-0:50:30 For somebody who is attuned to the light side of the Force, Qui-Gon sure tells a buncha lies in this film

-0:50:50 Does the midi-chlorian nonsense make sense to <u>anybody</u> besides Lucas?   Or is it just another stupid nonsense thing thrown in to try and tie this mess together?

-0:53:08 Now Qui-Gon is wagering a racing pod that doesn't belong to him...this guy knows <u>nothing</u> of boundaries!

-0:53:54 Why did Watto flap off without picking up his chance cube?

-0:55:35 "Two time winner Boles Roor."   I thought Watto said Sebulba always wins?

-0:56:30 Why do droids care if they get knocked into by another droid?

-0:58:20 Hate to nitpick a Hutt, but Jabba says "Begin the race," when he apparently means "Start your engines." Which could be a little confusing

-1:00:37 Shmi and company look at a monitor screen showing Annie's pod.   Where is the camera that is filming this image?   They have some helicopter chasing them?

-1:02:08 If it's only that pink lightning energy keeping the running engines from separating, it seems odd that there would be a second's pause between the lightning shutting down and the engines flying away

-1:02:35 Gee, you think a <u>droid</u> would be smart enough not to walk in front of a running jet engine

-1:04:56 As Anakin enters the canyon, there's a turn right ahead of him. So I thought it weird that he would accelerate--but next shot he's running down the straight canyon, no turn to be seen...

-1:05:50 Want a laugh? Start up the DVD commentary right here to listen to Lucas justify having an eight year-old controlling a hundred-mile-an-hour podracer by talking about how many 8 or 9 year-olds ride dirt-bikes and go-karts. Because that's the same thing. He actually uses the phrase "completely believable."

-1:06:29 ...and the kid sticks the <u>landing</u>? His pod was about two hundred feet in the air!

-1:06:58 I love when filmmakers tell on themselves. The visual effects supervisor, on the DVD commentary, points out right here--where you can see Sebulba's pod but nobody's in the cockpit!!

-1:09:18 Surprising that Sebulba bumps to a gentle stop, considering three seconds ago he was tied to an untethered racing jet engine

-1:09:36 The announcer: "The crowds are going nuts!" Did this guy learn English from Yoda? The word crowd implies plurality. There's just the one

-1:16:23 Continuity--Darth Maul's hood as he turns

-1:16:32 At least the podracer boys had goggles--Darth Maul takes off on his little scooter with no eye protection. Trust me, dear readers--above about 30 mph, he can't see!

-1:16:33 And he's really <u>cooking</u>, too! He drops over the edge of the ridge here, and <u>one second</u> later is visible on the canyon floor, about a mile or more away!!!

-1:16:47 Continuity, lightsabers

-1:22:05 Considering how high up this floating platform is, a <u>railing</u> might be a good idea

-1:26:00 "The boy's here to see Padme." Um, the boy has a name... (This guy is sooo gonna get Force-choked later!)

-1:29:08 If you've never noticed this--at this moment look for a delegation from E.T.'s planet in the lower-left senate pod

-1:30:40 "Fear leads to anger," Yoda says. I disagree--not that fear can't lead to anger, but it's only one avenue of many

-1:35:15 Much like happens in Episode 4, <u>A New Hope</u>, Artoo has a normally blue light that is <u>green</u> right here...and I think it's a nit!

-1:37:12 The holographic image turns, and keeps looking at the Trade Federation yahoos? Is somebody turning the camera focused on the yahoos, so that Sidious can still see <u>them</u>?

-1:40:00 They're trying to avert a war. Not a whole lotta time available. The Queen is locked out of her chambers--but she still finds time to change outfits/hairstyles! That classy dame

-1:44:47 Besides looking cool, is there a point to the walking holograph?

-1:48:42 On the commentary, Lucas explains away how foolish it is for the droid army to not be individually AI controlled but rather run by a master system. He says the Trade Federation yahoos feared their droids, if self-controlled, might become greedy like them. Which begs a different question--why would someone <u>program</u> a <u>droid</u> to become <u>greedy</u>? Why is that even a possibility??

-1:50:58 I don't care what anybody says, or how lame the rest of this movie is...that double-bladed lightsaber is <u>damn</u> cool

-1:51:10 Blaster bolts don't penetrate droideka shields. So why keep firing at them, wasting power packs?

-1:51:47 The ship's on automatic pilot? For a takeoff? I'm just gonna lump that together with the whole 9-year-old-starfighter-pilot nonsense and give the whole package the Will Award!!! (The helmet in the cockpit even fits him, sort of!)

-1:52:04 Continuity, Darth Maul

-1:52:05 Big lightsaber continuity here. Blade's over Maul's head, frame later its down in front of his chest

-1:52:20 More lightsaber continuity--and it keeps up like that, but this fight is so cool I'm gonna give it a pass unless I see something really off

-1:53:22 Why does the legless droid's gun go off every time Jar-Jar jumps on his chest?

-1:54:00 Little kid and his droid are out in deep space...still on autopilot? Do the Naboo leaders not trust these pilots at all?

-1:55:00 I don't buy the "ascension gun" bit. I don't believe the spikes bury into that ledge deep enough to support several hundred pounds of weight, and I don't buy that these folks could hang on to a slanted gun handle as they're being pulled up

-1:55:25 Lightsaber battle feet from insane purple generator energy.   What is it about the SW universe that nobody likes putting railings around thousand-foot falls?

-1:55:27 Obi-Wan falls off the platform going sideways, I don't know how one frame later he's in a swan dive

-1:55:28 The landing doesn't make sense either-- should've hit on his back, and much faster/harder

-1:56:00 Kenobi ignites his lightsaber and then starts running towards Jinn and Maul.   Somebody oughta tell him how dangerous that is to do

-1:56:18 What is the point of the closing/opening energy doors?   Besides creating dramatic tension?   (By the way, this is one of many, many moments during the commentary where the speaker talks about setting something up only to have Lucas change everything at the last minute.   Guy must be a peach to work for!)

-1:56:45 The Gungan shield generator is hit, explodes, and in the background the shield slooooowly rises and fades away.   Shouldn't it just disappear?

-1:57:55 Jar-Jar straddles a tank's gun barrel.   If that tank's been firing, I would expect that barrel to be very hot...

-1:58:00 Jar-Jar lucks out and fritzes the droid that pops out of the tank's hatch--and suddenly the tank is out of control. Why? Was that one droid running the thing?

-1:58:52 Anakin's fighter goes from hundreds-of-miles-per-hour to dead stop in far too short a time

-2:00:11 Lucky for us the droids were told to take prisoners, and not just kill everybody

-2:00:48 Okay, so if you buy that Padme/Amidala has a double that looks pretty much just like her, wouldn't it make sense--since the Trade Federation yahoos don't know which is which--to hold onto the one you have, as well as try and capture the other?

-2:02:04 How did Obi-Wan grab onto that shaft protrusion, given that he was falling away from the side? Oh, well, sure glad he did, I guess

-2:02:35 Anakin just happened to fire the bigger weapon, which just happened to hit the reactor core, which just happened to be out in the open hangar bay...I'm watching Star Wars I: the Amazing Coincidences!

-2:03:40 Does it make sense that the droid's head falls off, just because it is no longer being controlled from above?

-2:04:09 Lucky for Obi-Wan that Qui-Gon's lightsaber ignited on its own--since his hand doesn't touch the control stud.   Also lucky that Darth Maul is so goggled at Obi-Wan's leap that he doesn't slash him, which he has plenty of chance to do.

And, oh yeah--big continuity here.   Kenobi's lightsaber is pointed to one side, frame change, and it's up over his head

-2:04:25 Was surprised that Maul bit it--he seemed pretty cool, Darth Vader-type cool, and would have made a decent villain for the other two movies.   Except no, we've got Dooku and that coughing <u>robot</u>, don't we?   Sigh...

-2:04:38 Lucas, on the commentary, talks here about "the next six movies."   Um, unless you know something we don't, George, there's only five more!   Normally I would let that kind of thing go, but I'm mad at him

-2:07:22 Burning Jedi Master.   Bet that smells gooooood

-2:07:35 Kenobi turns towards Anakin, shot change-- he turns again

-2:07:43 "The council have granted me permission to train you."   No, the council <u>has</u> granted me permission to train you.   Learn English.   (And not from Yoda!)

-2:08:20 Mace Windu and Yoda are in the same room as Palpatine and they can't sense his evil?

-2:08:53 Please take note of new Padawan Anakin's required doofy hairdo

-2:09:08 Yoda here stands next to another big-eared fellow that looks like kinfolk.   Except big-ears looks human (except for the ears, I mean.)   So what's the deal?   They belong to the same Big-Ear Club?

Nice Touch Moment that I've never noticed before-- if you wait until the very last credits, you can hear one raspy Darth Vader breath as the music comes to an end!

But

These

Movies

Are

Still

Really

Really

Annoying!

#13:   Lord of the Rings II: The Two Towers

Ruminations: Part two of our journey through the movie-zation of one of the best stories ever!   The books are always better than the movies--but Jackson and company did pretty darn good.   This is the full-bore four-hour film-nerd extended version of the film, too, so gird your loins and off we go!

-0:01:44 The zoom from outside the mountain in to the Khazad-Dum bridge is of course CG, and strikes a false note for moi

-0:01:50 Continuity, Gandalf between shots

-0:02:10 It's just mean for the filmmakers to make us relive Gandalf's death (wink, wink)

-0:02:47 Does Galileo's law of motion on falling objects not apply in Moria?   How is Gandalf able to catch up with a sword that fell some seconds before him--not to mention a Balrog who fell before that?

-0:02:58 Continuity, Big G on the Balrog (more than once, so I'll just mention it this one time)

-0:03:33 Will Award!   Already?   Three minutes into the four hours worth of movie?   Yes...as much as I'm glad he somehow magically survived, the fact that Gandalf could fall roughly a mile and live, falling into water or not...that deserves my highest honor

-0:03:39 The slo-motion shot where they fall to the depths is ubercool, tho

-0:03:41 Except that the pair was well clear of the cavern ceiling, shot changes and they fall through the ceiling again!   Continuity!

-0:03:48 Did Frodo dream of Gandalf's fall, a la Harry Potter?   That fall was ages ago, why'd he just dream of it now?

-0:04:17 These Hobbits and their climbing skills! Bare hands, no carabiners, climbing right above one another even though one slip from Sam and they'll both fall!   What adventurers

-0:04:26 And on closeup, I submit that this thin rope would be really hard on one's hands

-0:04:38 Frodo risks his life for Sam's seasoning box? Truly terrible priorities.   Sam shoulda been more careful

-0:04:43 Oh!   It was just a three foot fall after all. Never mind

-0:05:00 Continuity, the box in Frodo's hands

-0:05:28 Speaking of boxes, what happened to the one Sam was given by Galadriel?   Read the books--it's a wonderful little bit that was totally cut from the movies

-0:06:00 Continuity--falling rope

-0:07:27 Continuity--the Lembas in Sam's hands

-0:07:40 Continuity, Sam biting his bread

-0:10:06 Continuity, Gollum as Sam pulls him away. And since Gollum is a completely digital character, you'd think they'd get it perfect

-0:10:18 Continuity, Sam and Gollum again

-0:10:40 Considering how vile and desperate Gollum is, lucky neither Hobbit lost an eye, or a finger, or anything vital in this fight

-0:10:44 Continuity, Frodo and Sting.   In the medium shot the hilt is near his head, in the closeup it's way behind him

-0:11:20 No nit here--just wanted to say that Andy Serkis' performance as Gollum/Smeagol is absolutely phenomenal.   For more fun, turn on the actors' DVD commentary (if you're nerd enough to have the extended version) to listen to Andy make jokes while switching between his own, Gollum and Smeagol's voices (live, no less!)

-0:12:23 Continuity, Gollum--he was moving his shoulders up, shot changes and he's suddenly moving down

-0:13:29 Hmm.   Frodo loosens the knot and pulls the rope off Gollum pretty easily.   Which would make sense if the knot was a slipknot--but if it was, why didn't it tighten when Gollum struggled?

-0:14:57 Hey, this orc leader was killed by Aragorn in the last movie!   What is this, the dude's brother?

-0:15:23 Nice of the orcs to speak English, huh?

-0:17:02 Lucky the brooch wasn't smushed under mud--be hard for Aragorn to find that

-0:17:30 Three days and nights chasing the orcs and still "no sign of our quarry but what bare rock can tell"? How far ahead did this group get while our heroes were sending Boromir to the depths?

-0:20:46 One orc is looking at another's face. It seems like a supervisor checking product, but what is he looking at? The orc's teeth? (Apparently Saruman has a good dental plan!)

-0:21:12 "The forest of Fangorn lies on our doorstep. Burn it." Oooh, you're gonna be sorry you said that...

-0:22:16 Continuity--the little girl is hoisted up onto the horse twice

-0:25:42 Wormtongue turns to look at Faramir twice. (By the by, Brad Dourif does an incredible job as Wormtongue!!)

-0:25:57 Just a note--this speech of Faramir's was Gandalf's in the book

-0:27:11 Continuity--our heroes running down the hill. They're much closer in the wide shot than in the medium

-0:28:14 Continuity, Merry was on his back a frame ago--now he's on his side

-0:28:16 How do the orcs get away with cutting branches in Fangorn? It's "perilous" to do that

-0:28:47 Right here Pippin talks about a forest near the Shire, and a story about trees coming alive. Read the book, seriously--in The Fellowship of the Ring there is a good hundred pages or so where the Hobbits actually traveled through said forest, and met those trees, and had to be rescued...none of which made the movie

-0:29:16 "What about them? They're fresh." That orc really think dividing up the two Hobbits will result in more than a mouthful apiece? Course, maybe he ain't planning on sharing

-0:30:10 "They think we have the Ring!" "Shh-- soon as they find out we don't, we're dead!" Yes, dear hobbits, do have this conversation in loud whispers when you are surrounded by enemies

-0:30:30 On top of everything else, orcs are cannibals? Nice

-0:31:20 Sure is lucky the hobbits don't get trampled during this fight

-0:31:32 "A red sun rises...blood has been spilled this night." Well, good morning to you too, Legolas!

-0:32:52 Continuity, Eomer's head as he dehorses

-0:32:56 Continuity, Gimli--two seconds ago there was a brown horse over his shoulder--now there's a black one there

-0:33:05 Does it really make any sense for Legolas the battle-hardened warrior to draw an arrow when there are already three dozen spears at our heroes throats?

-0:33:21 "I am Aragorn son of Arathorne.   This is Gimli son of Gloin, and Legolas of the woodland realm."   Is Leggy not the son of anybody that matters?   Or do elves just not care about heritage?

-0:33:46 Does it make sense for Eomer to tell Aragorn his life story?   About the king's sickness and being banished and all?   Especially when he thinks maybe our heroes are Saruman's spies?

-0:34:50 Here Eomer makes it sound as if Merry and Pippin are dead.   In the book he says "We found none but orcs."   Which would be nice for him to say here, since the missing children-sized hobbits were not among the slain. But he is having a difficult week

-0:35:00 Hey!   Here are three riderless horses--of which there is no evidence in earlier shots that showed the whole group of Rohirrim!   Where'd they come from?

-0:35:10 "Look for your friends, but do not trust to hope." Might be a good time to mention that there were only orcs among those killed, Eomer...

-0:35:20 I am not going to go back and count, but there seems to be twice as many Rohirrim riding away as encircled our heroes originally

-0:35:49 A pile of burned orc corpses. Betcha that smells gooooooood

-0:36:19 Continuity--Aragorn's hands as he drops to the ground

-0:36:30 "We failed them." Yeah, Gimli, pretty much--the fact that the hobbits are still alive has nothing to do with you three, that's for sure

-0:36:40 "A hobbit lay here." How can he tell that from random dirt?

-0:39:00 The filmmakers must have felt they needed more tension--this orc-chasing-the-hobbits-into-Fangorn stuff is not in the book. The first meeting with Treebeard happens in a much gentler way

-0:39:27 Interesting that Treebeard is very human-like. Two eyes, a nose, even a moustache

-0:39:37 How can Treebeard smush the orc?   The orc is on top of Merry!   Oh...wait...suddenly the orc is a couple of feet away and smushable.   Never mind

-0:40:38 Since Treebeard has been holding our friends for quite some time, and still thinks them to be little orcs, lucky for Merry and Pip that they haven't been crushed or thrown or something

-0:42:15 Continuity, Gollum as shot changes.   It's a fully digital effect which the filmmakers have full control over--no excuse for continuity errors!

-0:43:23 Continuity, Sam as Gollum eats the worm. When the shot cuts to closeup, the lembas is almost to his mouth, when it was by his chest before

-0:43:39 Doy, Frodo--didn't you see Gollum's reaction to the elvish rope?   What did you think their bread would do to him?

-0:45:24 Gollum, on the marsh faces: "All dead.   All rotten."   They do look dead, but I see no evidence of rotten-ness

-0:45:36 Continuity, CG Gollum

-0:46:09 Gollum says "Don't follow the lights," and "light little candles of their own," much like in the book-- except what lights?   I don't see any lights

-0:46:26 The filmmakers must have felt the need to add more conflict, because Frodo's dip in the marshes was <u>not</u> in the book

-0:47:00 Gollum drags Frodo out of the marsh--and Sam is not in sight?   Not right by his master's side, pushing Smeagol out of the way?   How odd

-0:49:49 How does the Black Rider's fell beast keep itself aloft, with wing beats only every coupla seconds?

-0:50:20 Lucky the Rider and his steed don't have very good eyesight--the hobbits ain't all that well hidden

-0:52:04 Why does Legolas suddenly speak to Aragorn in elvish?   Hoping to leave out Gimli for some reason?

-0:52:58 Yay, Gandalf is still alive!   Why did he sound like Saruman at first?   He doing his Christopher Lee impression just for fun?   (And lucky Legolas' arrow, Gimli's axe did no damage)

-0:53:58 "From the lowest dungeon to the highest peak I fought the Balrog."   Too bad they couldn't show us that battle--must have been quite the ballyhoo

-0:54:00 So lightning strikes Gandalf's sword, but doesn't hurt the wizard himself?   This guy sure is tough

-0:54:55 "I'd been sent back, until my task is done." The book says "Naked I was sent back..." and you can see that Gandalf doesn't have anything on, at least not up to his shoulders. Glad (a) that Peter Jackson didn't see fit to show us Big G's whole starkers self, and (b) that he found some robes somewheres

-1:02:00 If you care, this long monologue of Gandalf's about Sauron was pulled from the third book, near the end of the whole story, and stuck here for...well, for some reason

-1:03:39 Where'd this marching column come from, outside the gate of Mordor? No sight or sound of them a second ago

-1:03:51 Gollum makes like the trumpet blast hurts his ears, but look--he's not actually covering his ear, just sort of holding it

-1:04:03 While very cool, the Cave-Troll system of gate opening seems sketchy at best

-1:04:55 Did I already give away the Will Award? I did. Well, runner-up to the luck of Frodo and Sam that nobody sees them tumble down the hill, and that the elven cloaks just happen to magically look like a boulder so that a bad guy five feet away can't see, hear or smell them...

I mean, baddies are <u>looking</u> right at the hill as they struggle on it!

-1:05:45 The hem of the magic cloak was an inch or two above the rocks, we saw from the inside. Now Frodo throws it off (only three seconds after the bad guys turn away, no less) and it has conveniently been rocked into place before he does

-1:05:53 Continuity, Sam digging out of the rocks. He was half-free, then the shot changed and he's almost buried again

-1:07:55 It's also pretty lucky that the hobbits and their little friend can scramble back <u>up</u> the rocky hill without being spotted, shot at from the walls, etc.

-1:10:28 The filmmakers must have thought we needed more conflict--this captured-by-a-strange-Ent-in-Fangorn bit never happened in the book, though it is similar to what was cut from <u>The Fellowship of the Ring</u>. (Surprised Tom Bombadil doesn't show up to help!)

-1:11:10 Treebeard needs to make up his mind. When he left the hobbits alone last night, he said nothing would harm them.   Now he says the forest is unsafe

-1:11:47 "There be no Entings for a terrible long time."   I am curious how Ents get, um, "busy" and make these Entings

-1:15:10 The scene between Wormtongue and Eowyn is not in the book either, but I won't complain--it's very powerful, and well played by the actors.   It's obvious how Eowyn longs for any touch, even that of Grima Wormtongue, if only for a moment

-1:18:03 Continuity--as the doors shut, Gandalf was turning his head, then the shot changes and he's not looking anymore.   And why does everybody always turn to look when doors shut behind them anyway?

-1:19:07 The filmmakers must've thought we needed more conflict--the fistfight in Theoden's hall is not in the book

-1:21:15 Theoden's reversal is very well done

-1:22:25 The design of Theoden's sword hilt is pretty, and fits the horse theme--but that short roundedness would probably be impractical in battle

-1:22:50 Wow! A moment of silence to honor the poor stuntman who had to fall down those stone steps!

-1:22:53 Continuity as Wormy turns over

-1:23:19 What right does Aragorn have to stop Theoden from killing Wormtongue? Mind your own business, Strider! The part Wormy plays in Return of the King didn't make it into the movie anyway

-1:26:13 "That I should live to see the last days of my house." There's other things to worry about, but it's not like Theoden couldn't try and make himself another heir...

-1:26:20 "No parent should have to bury their child." It's pretty easy to tell the lines Tolkien didn't write--like everything in this scene. I'm pretty sure he would have said something like "No father should have to bury his son," which makes more sense considering Middle-Earth culture

Yes, I'm a geek

-1:30:13 "Three hundred lives of men I've walked this earth..." Sheesh, Gandalf is like, Methuselah

-1:30:27 Big G rides away, staff in hand. Where'd that naked sword he was holding go?

-1:30:58 The Horse-whisperer scene ain't in the book either

-1:32:28 "Turn this fellow free. He has seen enough of war." There Aragorn goes again, giving orders where he has no authority. The Rohirrim need every good horse they can get, dude

-1:33:29 Wormtongue gives a detailed description of Aragorn's ring. When in the world did he get a good look at that?

-1:39:09 The Gollum vs. Smeagol debate is really, really, really well done!

-1:39:29 But...unless this is all inside the poor guy's head, there are nits aplenty. Like here, where Smeagol has his hands over his ears, and Gollum does not. There's more, but you get the idea

-1:41:04 I'm amazed the hobbits don't wake up during Smeagol's cavorting

-1:43:30 "The dark one is gathering all armies to him." Since when is Smeagol the fount of all Sauron knowledge?

-1:45:10 Frodo says "C'mon, Sam," and there's nobody behind him. He turns around and one second later runs into Faramir's soldier? Ninjas, these guys are!

-1:45:21 Continuity, Sam as the sword is at his throat

-1:45:40 Frodo: "We are bound on a secret mission." If it's a secret, don't <u>talk</u> about it, short stuff!

On to disk two...

-0:00:34 Continuity as Gimli falls off his horse

-0:02:10 You're probably tired of this by now, but the scene with Eowyn, Aragorn and the stew isn't in the book--and is a little forced, in my opinion

-0:02:40 Huh? Aragorn is eighty-seven years old? He just said so...wow! That's some exercise regimen he has!

-0:03:42 Finally!   It's been over two hours and this is the first we see of Liv Tyler!   Doesn't Peter Jackson know what we came for?

-0:07:13 I'm all for the extended movies, I want to see as much of this world as I can, but these Arwen/Aragorn scenes (also, dare I say, not in the books) really drag things down

-0:08:43 Some sharp warriors these guys are--the orc-ridden-Warg is fully visible on the cliff about fifty feet away, but they don't see him?

-0:08:50 By the by, the whole Warg battle and Aragorn supposedly being killed, none of this is in the book. The filmmakers must have decided we needed more conflict

-0:12:05 Gimli braces himself, pushes against the Warg/orc combo lying on top of him, then another Warg peeks over--standing on the first two.   And Gimli is <u>still</u> pushing this off his chest?   Dude sure is strong

-0:12:30 Continuity as Aragorn is knocked to the ground

-0:21:30 Yay, Aragorn's not dead!

-0:23:53 As much as Aragorn and Arwen belong together, I gotta admit, Elrond has a point about how he'll die and she'll go on living

-0:24:59 So all of Middle-Earth stands on the brink of war--meanwhile Elrond and his kinfolk are just going to bug out?   Sure, Elrond was there for the battle with Sauron thousands of years ago, he's paid some dues, but still--thanks a lot, pointy ears!

-0:26:44 "Frodo begins to understand the quest will claim his life.   You have foreseen this."   Um, nuh-uh!

-0:28:30 Nice touch, Faramir and friend consulting a map straight from the first pages of the books

-0:33:33 Continuity, Denethor.   He hugs Boromir, and when the camera is behind him, his left hand is at Boromir's shoulder, but when the camera is behind Boromir, Daddy's hand is around his neck

-0:38:30 For swimming in the Forbidden Pool the penalty is death (they really oughta put up signs), but since you, Frodo, whom I've never met before and suspect of being a spy, say not to kill this creature we'll make an exception just this once

-0:42:20 Faramir was able to deduce that "My Precious!" was the One Ring?   Call him Sherlock Holmes

...and by the way, you may not care but in the book Sam lets slip about the Ring, Faramir doesn't learn it from Gollum

-0:43:51 And in the book Faramir lets Frodo leave from the cave, he doesn't drag him to Osgiliath.   In fact all of the scenes that take place in Osgiliath are not in the book, and in my opinion add little to the movie

-0:44:50 Wait--Aragorn is riding Beregond, or whatever that horse's name is?   I thought he said "let him go, he's seen too much of war?"!

-0:45:18 I know Aragorn has been busy, but seems like he might have taken five minutes to bind the open wound on his shoulder

-0:49:28 Continuity--Treebeard just put his weight on his right foot, shot changes and he puts his right foot down

-0:50:08 Have I mentioned that the Ents are very extremely well done?

-0:54:21 Where in the world is this God-light shining into the king's chamber coming from?

-0:55:02 We see here a shot of a kid, looks about eleven, being helmeted.   What's the cutoff?   There was a boy back in the caves that looked this old, waving goodbye as daddy went off to war...

I also submit that it makes little sense to send anyone so young out to war--regardless of whether the kid can hold a sword, he is not going to be any real use in battle. And worse, those around him will definitely lose heart, seeing a child cut down!

-0:58:50 Yay!   Reinforcements!   From...Egypt, apparently

-1:00:30 Okay, it's funny, but Gimli the very proud dwarf couldn't find <u>anything</u> to stand on, see over the wall?

-1:00:35 And what's the crazy God-light shining from behind everybody? It ain't the moon

-1:02:55 Aragorn, as usual, looks like he is going to give the signal to fire. Isn't that Theoden's job? Who put Strider in charge of the world?

-1:03:09 Why, this cute little kid with the huge eyes looks very much like a hobbit we saw in the first film! (wink, wink)

-1:03:31 The old guy shoots by mistake and--oh no!-- battle is joined. Um...what else could possibly have happened? That's what these orcs came here for

-1:04:03 Legolas tells his fellow elves where the orcs' armor is weak. Wow--is this information he should have shared <u>much</u> earlier, and to all his kin, and not just to the couple within earshot on either side. He doesn't even raise his voice!

-1:05:25 Wilhelm Scream! (Google it)

-1:06:10 In case you're wondering--the game, where Legolas and Gimli keep track of their kills and try to outdo one another?   That is straight from the book

-1:07:56 Just thought of this now, but lucky that Treebeard understands English!

-1:08:51 And here comes the representative from Middle-Earth with the Olympic torch!

-1:09:06 Aragorn makes a huge deal about killing the torch bearer, as if there aren't a thousand orcs around who could pick up the torch and finish the job

-1:09:11 The torchbearer was hit with at least two arrows, but here where he jumps into the tunnel, I can't spot any sticking out of him

-1:09:15 Sometimes   things   happen   so   fast, filmmakers show us several angles.   We see the Helm's Deep explosion three times

-1:10:00 Are four old guys leaning against the inside of the gate really going to make any difference in stopping the ramming team?

-1:10:32 Continuity as Gimli jumps off the wall

-1:10:56 Continuity as Aragorn runs down the hill (slo-motion makes my job so easy.)   His sword is on the left, then a frame later it's on the right

-1:11:07 Really?   Legolas skateboarding down the steps on a shield?   ...okay

-1:11:40 This made me upset in the theaters, and I'm still horked--it wasn't Merry who talked the Ents into helping, they decided to attack Isengard on their own!   This version gives Merry more lines, but takes away the honor of the Ents

yes, I'm a geek

-1:15:40 When'd Aragorn get in here?   He was outside the wall thirty seconds ago

-1:16:35 Wow, that was a mighty toss for an eighty-seven year-old

-1:18:31 Sure lucky for Aragorn and Gimli that nobody tried shooting them while they were being hauled up the wall

-1:23:34 Ents are cool--and this Last March of the Ents truly fantastic

-1:23:50 When what really matters is getting the Ring to daddy, I'm not sure why Faramir goes to Osgiliath. But since Tolkien didn't write any of this, maybe I shouldn't expect it to make much sense

-1:25:10 Some weird field is on Osgiliath that everything falls in slo-motion. The rocks coming down in the establishing shot, the tower pieces after the rock hits them...

-1:28:36 Gimli goes to blow the horn of Helm's Deep? Seems like that's something one of the Rohirrim should be doing

-1:30:09 The Rohirrim are great horsemen, but still...that's an awfully steep slope to have several hundred horses running down

-1:30:53 Stones fall slowly in Isengard, too

-1:31:18 Merry and Pippin throw stones--which they got from where? Is Treebeard picking up stones to hand to the hobbits?

-1:33:18 Sam sees Frodo walking like a zombie, towards the Nazgul, and does nothing to try and stop him?

-1:34:15 Did I give out the Will Award? I did. Well, third runner-up. Frodo pulled out the Ring right in front of the Ringwraith, who has no thought beyond getting said Ring to his master...and yet because his steed has one arrow in him, pulls away, leaving Frodo and Sam alone.

Maybe if Tolkien had written any of this, it would've made more sense...

-1:34:22 Continuity as Sam hits the ground

-1:34:50 And hey, isn't Sting supposed to glow blue when orcs are around?

-1:36:09 Did the Ents release another river? Or did Jackson decide the flooding of Isengard was so cool we deserved to see it a second time? (It is cool, mind you...)

-1:41:00 "Do you think we should share it with Treebeard?"   Share the pipeweed?   A <u>tree</u> smoking? Somehow I doubt it, fellas

-1:47:00 With all of the trekking around in the wilderness, with lots of exercise and little food, I'm surprised that Sam is still that fat...

#14: Jurassic Park

Ruminations: what's a movie from the nineties doing way up here in the top fifteen?   From back when they didn't do all the special-effects in computers?

It's a great film, from a better book, and it very much deserves to be here.   Some of the reviews I had to do were with teeth-gritted.   This one I sat back and smiled.

And found some very interesting stuff I'd never seen before!

Which is what it's all about, after all...

-0:00:11 Remarkably cloudless sky in that Universal logo--Earth's spinning awfully fast, too

-0:01:17 Muldoon the dinosaur tracker guy stands there, gun in hand, dramatically lit from below.   Um...why are there lights on the ground?

-0:01:30 And where did they go?   No lights on the ground in wide shot

-0:02:35 Why is some poor schlub expected to lift the gate by hand, of this raptor prison?   Why isn't there some mechanical way to do so? (Answer: because somebody had to get chomped right from the start)

-0:02:45 The lights changed from red to green, indicating a lock of some kind. If this is an electronic, magnetic, tough type of lock--which it should be, to deal with a raptor--how does the V-rap get it unlocked so simply?

-0:02:58 Continuity, Muldoon--he gets up to help the Being-Chomped, then shot changes and he gets up again

-0:03:45 Just what does Juanito say in Spanish as the lawyer comes up on the boat? "Bet you a thousand pesos he falls."

-0:04:24 Continuity, bloodsucking lawyer as shot changes

-0:04:45 The lawyer is let into the mine? Hard-hatless? Really?

-0:05:04 Does it make a whole lot of sense to get everybody away from their jobs to shine light on a piece of amber--when the mine foreman could just take ten steps and look at it outside?

-0:05:32 From what (little) I know of archaeological studies, these students are brushing off those bones mighty fast, and with far too little care

-0:06:30 If this computer dude was expecting an "immediate" return--why didn't he have the monitor turned on?

-0:07:00 Grant gets all this crap because he breaks the computer--if the monitor fuzzes because he just barely touches it, I put the blame on the computer geek, not him (it's not like he sat down at the keyboard and started typing in commands, after all)

-0:07:43 The scene where Grant scares the little punk kid is fun, and gets some important velociraptor exposition out of the way.   It's good writing.   But where are this kid's parents?   They just let him mouth off like that? (I know, lots of kids would and do mouth off like that.   But how many of those kids are on archaeological dig sites?)

...and oh, by the way--sources tell me actual discovered velociraptor fossils are roughly turkey-sized.   Not ten feet tall

-0:08:00 "You think his visual acuity is based on movement, like T-Rex."   When was <u>that</u> proven?   Grant talks like it's scientific fact.   Nobody's ever seen a tyrannosaurus rex, so how can he be so sure?

-0:08:20 Grant goes on about velociraptor attack strategy--how, again, does he have any idea what that strategy would have been?

-0:08:43 If I was the kid's parent, I would have a bit of a problem with Grant slashing with his v-rap claw right close to my boy's tummy like that

-0:09:58 During the five seconds that Grant runs over to the copter, old cane-bearing Hammond had enough time to get all the way down to the trailer?

-0:10:14 This is fun--I laughed out loud.   Never noticed this before, but know how you tell they filmed an exterior on-location and the interior on a soundstage?   One way is when the outside door handle is on the left side (so it opens left-to-right) and the inside door handle is on the right side (it opens right-to-left)!   Watch as Grant opens the trailer door!

-0:11:20 Continuity, Hammond's hands.   He's rubbing the glass, shot changes, and his hands are spread

-0:12:27 Grant is so interested in Hammond's pitch that he doesn't care about the dust all over his face?   It's bugging me, is all I'm saying...

-0:13:50 Dodgson stops and looks around--he can't see the beached whale in a Hawaiian shirt that is Dennis Nedry?   Guy's probably visible from space in that shirt

-0:14:30 Continuity--Nedry's hands on the bag as shot changes

-0:14:40 Dodgson resets the embryo canister, shot changes and he resets it again

-0:14:51 It's a nice gag, Nedry wiping the shaving cream onto the pie--and it's further good writing, showing his character--but what's a table full of desserts sitting out in the open for, anyway?

-0:14:57 Continuity, Nedry's hands

-0:15:32 "So you two dig up dinosaurs?"   Malcolm waited until they were five minutes from the island before striking up conversation?

-0:16:37 Okay, let's think about the helicopter seating.   We've seen out the window as Hammond and Malcolm argue, and Hammond is clearly sitting with his back to the cockpit.   (Unless the chopper is flying backwards, which earlier establishing shots and sheer logic indicate it ain't.)   So when Hammond looks out the window and says "There it is," he's looking at an island the chopper is at best flying parallel to, and at worst <u>away from</u>!   What is this pilot's problem?   Or is Hammond confused?

-0:16:58 The chopper flies very dramatically through the gorgeous canyons.   Considering how few travel options there are to and from this island, wouldn't it make a <u>lot</u> more sense for the chopper to travel up high, over the peaks, where there's a much lesser chance of running into anything?

-0:13:12 I don't buy the "bad wind shear" explanation for how they have to drop so fast, and I don't buy the inside jumping around as accurate helicopterial turbulence

-0:18:26 At 18:10 we watched the chopper land, and the jeeps were parked right by the pad. Now we see a jeep backing up to the pad. Did the drivers start driving away and have to come back? Why?

And what sense does it make to put a helicopter pad five feet above a lake? I really don't think this spot is all that safe in the event of, say, a monsoon...

-0:18:59 The sign <u>says</u> "Danger, 10,000 volts." There's even a picture of a hand being lightning-ed through. Yet these guys close the doors with their bare hands? Huh?

-0:19:25 I think the lawyer misspeaks here. He's talking about the investors being concerned, and how he's their representative for a serious investigation. Then he says, "48 hours from now, if they're not convinced, I'm not convinced." Shouldn't that be the other way around?

-0:19:48 Continuity--as the jeep stops, Grant is looking off to the side. Then the shot changes and Grant is sitting back, facing forward.

And where'd Ellie get a leaf from, anyway?

-0:20:12 In all the fuss about the dinosaurs, I never thought about how they have prehistoric plants on this island. How'd they get <u>those</u>? They find some prehistoric deer trapped in amber, clone the contents of their stomachs?

-0:20:13 Continuity, Grant's hand on Ellie's head

-0:20:15 Grant's reaction to seeing the brachiosaurus is classic, and right on. But I have a Peripheral Vision Problem with the whole thing. The jeeps drove up to this site and stopped, and only now, they're noticing this giant dinosaur?

-0:20:28 Steven Spielberg, Michael Crichton, and John Williams. A match made in heaven

-0:21:13 Three seconds ago we looked up past Grant's shoulder at the dino--he was maybe fifteen feet away. (Far too close, but anyway) Now suddenly all three are fifty feet away. When did that happen?

-0:21:19 I'm not sure what Brachy is accomplishing, going up on his hind legs. It only seems to put his head about three feet higher--and there's plenty of leaves around anyway

-0:22:07 "Welcome, to Jurassic Park." I'm told the accurate title would be <u>Mesozoic Park</u>, given the animals inhabiting the island. But anyway

-0:22:33 Grant ain't the greatest scientist. These animals have somehow been recreated millions (or is it billions? Trillions? I forget how much time evolutionists need now to make their increasingly wilder theories fit any sort of reality) of years after extinction, and Grant talks about how "They do move in herds." As though what he's seeing is the definitive answer for all of the dinosaur questions. But scientifically, the animals are in a situation they've never been in before. How can anything they do be considered authentic to their original environments?

Or am I over-thinking things again?

-0:23:19 They've got the real thing outside. What point is there to the collection of museum-quality fossils in this atrium?

-0:23:55 This "ride", that explains the park and how we have dinosaurs. It's brilliantly written, Michael Crichton was a genius...but does it make any sense for Hammond to explain the secret of his dinosaurs like this? Sure, to Malcolm and Grant and Ellie, he needs them to endorse the park--but this setup makes it seem as though everybody who visits here will learn how its done.

Sheesh, who needs industrial espionage when the guy's giving his secrets away!

-0:24:05 "Hello, John!"   The video screen talks to the real Hammond.   So...Hammond is going to stand here <u>every</u> time the ride goes through, to answer back?   This guy needs to prioritize

-0:25:24 When the miners found the amber-coated mosquitoes, the ones they got blood out of (brilliant, I cannot state that enough), how did they luck out and get the right kind?   What if all they got was Mesozoic wild pig, or just a bunch of the little chicken-sized ones?

-0:26:41 "And virtual-reality displays show us the gaps in the genetic sequence."   Is there <u>really</u> any point to this guy with the VR gloves and helmet besides an attempt to seem cool and futuristic?   (Anybody else remember when Virtual Reality was the wave of the future?   Here's hoping this 3-D craze follows VR real soon--I'm sick of having it shoved down my throat)

-0:27:08 Is Hammond also going to join every tour to press the button for the moving part?

-0:27:33 "Those people are the real miracle workers of Jurassic Park."   Just the kinda job I want to have, a new group of tourists gawking at me every ten minutes

-0:27:52 So the three of them working together can lift the gate?   During the ride?   Wonder if that works at real amusement parks...

-0:28:23 Nobody questions the visitors, or asks why they aren't in clean suits, or anything...

-0:28:32 The robot arm is turning the eggs.   Never thought about it before, but how does it turn the eggs <u>it can't reach</u>?   The ones on the other side of the table?

-0:28:57 Continuity, eggshell breaking

-0:29:21 Continuity, newly hatched v-rap as shot changes

-0:29:28 "They imprint on the first creature they come in contact with.   Helps them to trust me."   Yeah, Hammond, you tell yourself that when the velociraptors come after you

-0:30:22 How'd the robot arm know Grant was touching the eggshell?   And the robot gets pissy about egg handling, but doesn't mind that Grant later has the v-rap in his hands?

-0:31:00 I like Jeff Goldblum.   What happened to him?   Seems like I haven't seen him in ages

-0:34:02 And the previously cow-holding harness comes up, chewed, battered and cow-less.   Seems like a very expensive thing to replace harnesses daily like that

-0:34:45 Continuity, lawyer's hands

-0:35:08 Editors must just loooove scenes where there are constantly moving images in the background. These slide projectors changing every three or so seconds makes continuity just impossible.   Kudos to whoever was on deck because the scene started several minutes ago, and this is the first one I caught--the slide behind the lawyer changes instantly between the last shot and this one

-0:35:14 And once again here

-0:36:01 The slide behind Hammond reads "Jurassic Tennis."   Is this a nature preserve, or a resort?

-0:38:06 Now the slide behind Hammond is static, hasn't changed for some time.   Who told the projector guy that it was the end of the scene, and he should hold on that one?

-0:39:00 The cars run electrically, but they're not in any way connected to the rail on the ground...I don't think that's gonna work

-0:39:21 Continuity--Grant   passes   Timmy,   shot changes and he passes him again

-0:40:37 "Ay-yai-yai, why didn't I build a land dock?" Actually, Hammond, that's a <u>great</u> question.   Is everybody visiting this island theme park going to come in by 6 person helicopter?   There seems to be no way for large boats to get to the island--and how do the velociraptor cows get offloaded?   They come in by chopper too?

-0:40:50 Aww, look at young Samuel L. Jackson there.   Only person in this cast who's still working!

-0:41:04 Are more cars going to be added to the tour, or will only ten people get to go at a time?   This park sure will need to charge a lot

-0:42:00 Oy--want a drinking game suggestion? Take a slug every time Hammond says "We spared no expense."

-0:42:20 "Caution--keep windows up!"   Seriously? Since there are dinos out there that can spit venom, why is it even possible to roll the car windows <u>down</u>?

-0:42:31 The dino-crazed kid (and who can blame him?) is crowding his older sister for a view out the window. I was 10 once--I can't imagine why Tim doesn't get into the way back of the car, where he'd have a window all to himself (Of course, in real-life the guy driving the supposedly computer-driven car is back there, under a cover!)

-0:43:20 Continuity--Nedry lifts his can twice

-0:46:25 I know storms in Costa Rica can come up fast, but it wasn't raining <u>one frame</u> ago, so...that's really fast

-0:46:55 And now car windows all dry! Crazy tropical weather

-0:47:24 Continuity--Malcolm reaches past Ellie twice

-0:48:16 Continuity, Malcolm's hands

-0:48:20 Not only do the windows roll down, but the doors open! That seems safe

-0:48:32 Both doors close just after Ellie gets out. So she bothered shutting both of them as she went after Grant? That was nice of her

-0:48:43 Grant got out of the car to cut across an open field. Ellie followed. Now the monitor shows the cars (lucky there was a camera nearby, huh?) and they're all getting out, Grant and Ellie are next to the cars and there's trees everywhere! Why'd the first two come back, and where'd these trees come from?

-0:50:13 So the dinosaurs have a vet? I suppose it makes sense that somebody's there to take care of them, but how does he have the first <u>clue</u> what he's doing?

-0:51:01 The vet comes over and hands Ellie a flashlight so they can talk diagnosis. What does <u>she</u> know from treating sick dinosaurs?

-0:51:26 The vet didn't see that the Triceratops' pupils are dilated? Her pupils are the size of saucers. This guy is terrible!

-0:51:32 "That's pharmacological. From local plant life." How in the name of all that is holy does she know all this? Sure, she's an expert on dinosaurs and fossilized plants, but bones are <u>all</u> she's ever had to work with!

-0:54:55 Continuity, L. Jackson--turns his head twice

-0:55:36 As Nedry begins his skullduggery, the StopWatch Go box on his screen is black in the wider shot, where he synchronizes his wristwatch with the computer, then it's grey (turning to black) on the closeup. Also, he hits the button, the shot cuts to closeup and a second later things start running. What's with the delay from hitting the button and go?

-0:57:19 Dodgson talked to Nedry about getting an embryo from all fifteen species of dinosaur. But the canister Nedry is holding sure looks like it has only <u>twelve</u> embryo slots!

-0:58:45 So Nedry is on the main route through the park--that's the <u>best</u> way to get to the boat dock? Seems poorly planned--that's what maintenance tunnels are for

-0:59:43 And the arrow on the sign can point in either direction?   That's seriously poorly designed

-1:00:35 And of course the cars stopped <u>right</u> outside the Tyrannosaur's paddock, right by that poor goat we saw earlier.   Also, since the tour was cut short, I wonder how exactly they got the cars (you know, the ones on the electric rail) <u>turned around</u> and facing the opposite direction!

-1:01:21 There just <u>happens</u> to be night-vision goggles in designer colors?   Convenient

-1:01:24 Continuity, lights on goggles as shot changes

-1:01:38 Was Grant's water bottle under the seat, like Tim's night-vision goggles, or did he bring that with?   He wasn't carrying anything earlier that I noticed

-1:01:56 Lex turns twice--continuity

-1:02:16 The water vibrations, signaling the approaching dinosaur, is fantastic and a classic movie shot. But...why is the T-rex stomping one foot at a time, in such a dramatic fashion?   He hung up on vines, or stomping in rain puddles maybe?

-1:03:56 Dramatic shot of the fence bowing out, presumably from the weight of T-rex's tiny little arms. But...there's no dinosaur in the shot.   This seems wrong

-1:04:20 Please allow me to pause in my nitpicking to remark upon the INCREDIBLE job they did making the T-rex come to life!   Astounding!

-1:04:29 "Keep absolutely still.   His vision's based on movement."   I've said it before, but--how does he know?

-1:04:42 Twenty seconds ago the T-rex passed between the two cars.   Now suddenly it's back on the right side of Grant and Malcolm.   Did Rexy make a loop, or something?

-1:04:49 Continuity, "Turn the light off!"   Lex just moved it towards the right side of the car, shot changes and she's pointing it straight out the back window

-1:05:19 The T-rex eye dilation is possibly one of the best shots in the history of cinema

-1:05:30 Sound continuity?   The T-rex is roaring her little heart out, shot changes and the sound cuts off just like that.   Seems odd

-1:05:42 Rexy tilts the car a bit, shot cuts inside and though the kids are screaming, the car is level.   Another shot inside and it's still level, cut back outside and car is tilted

-1:05:56 Continuity, the hands on the plastic panel with Rexy on the other side.   (And the screams of the actors are real, because that panel was <u>not</u> supposed to pop off on set)

-1:05:59 Second shot of the panel, Rexy is right there, then we cut to a POV shot and the dinosaur has reared back, between frames?

-1:06:10 There was also a piece broken off a moment ago, but in this shot you can just barely see that the panel has magically repaired itself

-1:06:12 Rexy has been attacking the kids for almost a minute, and the Grant/Malcolm team are just <u>sitting</u> there? Come on, heroes!!

-1:06:22 This is funny--if you freeze frame here, as the car falls on its roof, you can not only see an unexplained black line running from the side of the car out of frame, but you can also <u>clearly</u> see a C-stand with a light on it, not quite hidden behind a <u>potted plant</u>!!

-1:06:32 Did the goat fulfill Rexy's hunger pangs? Why is he attacking tires, and not fresh children morsels?

-1:06:41 And only <u>now</u> does Grant start taking action. I guess the kids are in sufficient trouble now, huh?

-1:06:59 Continuity, flare as shot changes

-1:07:03 Continuity, flare as shot changes

-1:07:38 Boy, you just can't get good workers these days.   That entire restroom fell apart, walls and all, revealing the lawyer on the potty!   What are the odds?

-1:07:42 Continuity, lawyer McNugget

-1:07:50 I'm tempted to make a lawyers-versus-human-beings joke, but I'll let it pass.   RIP, dude

-1:08:10 Continuity as Grant struggles to restrain Lex

-1:08:14 And continuity again--suddenly his left hand is on her shoulder

-1:08:22 And again--after Rexy blows off Grant's hat, their heads are right next to each other.   Next shot we see Grant and Lex but no dino

-1:08:26 And again!   As Rexy turns the vehicle, Grant and Lex fall down--shot changes and they fall down again

-1:09:00 Wait, whoa, now they're by this cliff? What happened to the firm ground the goat was standing on, and which Rexy stepped over the barrier on?   Where'd this fershlugginer <u>cliff</u> come from?

-1:09:11 The car was sinking into the mud.   How'd Rexy get it up onto this three foot barrier?

-1:09:38 Well, if Tim was in that car that just fell in the tree, he's dead--or at least seriously injured.   He's not walking away from that one

-1:10:31 "Ah-ah-ah, you didn't say the magic word!" We hear this now--why didn't we hear it for the past thirty seconds?   (not that I'm complaining)

-1:10:59 Nedry crashes against a berm of earth--shot changes and the front of the jeep isn't against anything

-1:11:12 "There's the road!"   And with a very convenient East Dock sign, too!

-1:11:24 I swear the sound-effect guy put in a "fweee!" like in Bugs Bunny cartoons when Nedry slips and falls on his backside.   Maybe it's just me

-1:11:29 Nedry rolls over twice (continuity) when he hits the road

-1:11:48 Maybe this isn't a nit, maybe Nedry is just stupid.   But he goes, like, a hundred yards into the forest to put the cable around a tree, when there seem to be a number of closer trees to choose from

-1:12:06 "You got time, you got time, you can do it!" Nedry was begging the dock guy for fifteen minutes earlier, and that was before all of his shenanigans.   He still has time to catch his boat?   Really?

-1:13:19 In addition to the headlights, and the roof lights, there is a light shining through the back window of the jeep--and I have <u>no</u> idea what would be causing that

-1:13:50 Continuity, the slime on Nedry's face.   It was just up at his eyes, then he turns, shot changes and it's all over his face

-1:13:52 Continuity--he turns twice to get into the car

-1:13:54 Continuity--Nedry falls with arms extended, shot changes and his arms are at his sides

-1:14:14 That light behind the jeep is still there-- what is that?   Oh, well.   RIP, Nedry

-1:14:31 Boy, the editor was not having the greatest day!   Continuity--Lex is right behind Grant, almost touching him, then shot changes and she's several feet away

-1:15:10 The car fell right down the retaining wall into this tree, right?   It didn't fly away over the park.   So the retaining wall should be right behind the tree, right?

...so where'd it go...?

-1:15:26 Grant's got the whole tree to use for climbing--so he climbs up right <u>under</u> the car?   Moron

-1:15:40 A moment ago water was falling from the tree--suddenly it's all dry

-1:16:18 Awful bright in this tree--I suppose the car headlights bouncing off tree branches is providing all this illumination?

-1:17:05 Grant and Tim have the whole tree to use for climbing--so they climb down right <u>under</u> the car? Double morons

-1:17:07 Grant turned the wheel helping Tim out--when did it get all straight again?

-1:17:44 Nice of the car to fall in such a controlled, gentle way, since these two are still stupidly climbing right under it

-1:18:00 When the car touches earth, it just <u>barely</u> touches it, meaning obviously the tree is still supporting the weight somehow.   Cut to the shot where the car falls over--and it's obviously not

-1:19:43 Ellie sees the other car, shot changes and they're down where the car came out of the tree.   Is there a convenient set of stairs that Grant just missed, or did they climb down on cables?   To save time mentioning it later, they sure get back up to Malcolm fast as well

-1:20:14 Rexy's doing that slow-stomping thing again

-1:21:10 Since Rexy can easily keep up with the jeep, I am agog that nobody else gets bit or otherwise injured. Guess that lawyer's tiding her over

-1:22:27 Tim sure bounced back fast from the T-Rex scare!   He's   already   excited   about   seeing Brachiosauruseseses

-1:22:32 Big light behind this tree--which is what, exactly?   Somebody else have a car in a tree behind our heroes?

-1:23:21 Continuity--Grant settles back against the tree twice

-1:23:50 "What are you and Ellie gonna do if you don't have to dig up dinosaur bones anymore?"   Sure, because now that we've genetically engineered more dinosaurs, nobody is going to care about the real ones of the past!

-1:25:09 Hammond eating the ice cream is another example of how well this film was written.   The scriptwriter doesn't have somebody say "Hammond, you sure are clueless and naïve..." they show us.   The power's out, the food going to go bad, and what is Hammond eating?   Ice cream.   Like the little child he is.   Brilliant

-1:25:40 "Who better to get the children through Jurassic Park than a dinosaur expert?" Yes, because archaeology translates to wilderness survival so readily

-1:26:26 Hammond talks about his Flea Circus. I can visualize a motorized high-wire act, but clown fleas? Fleas on Parade? What did he do for the parade, play bouncy music over an empty box?

-1:28:21 Ooh, take a drink! He said "spared no expense" again!

-1:29:08 The Brachiosaur is as well-done as the Tyrannosaur. The effects are truly top-of-the-line, and since I know they weren't all digitally done, I have even more respect for the filmmakers

-1:29:28 Continuity (tired of that word yet?)--the Brachiosaur started moving away, shot changed and it moves again

-1:29:47 Continuity as Lex moves out to touch Brachy

-1:29:52 Dinosaurs sneeze? Did not know that

-1:30:40 "But Grandpa said all the dinosaurs were girls." When did Grandpa say that? Assuming the dinosaur park was a surprise, did they all go on the ride again, before jumping in the cars?

-1:30:47 And it's time for the Will Award!   Yaaay! So all the genetic dinosaurs out here are females, right? And they used amphibian DNA to repair gaps in the DNA code, right?   So...because there is one species of frog that in a single-sex environment can switch teams to, erhm, get it done, so to speak--that explains everything!   Because there's bits of amphibian DNA filling in the sequencing gaps, that makes it possible for the dinosaurs, who are so much like tiny frogs, to also change sex if they want!   It's not at all ridiculously implausible if you think about it!   (I swear, folks who believe in evolution will swallow absolutely anything)

-1:31:05 Our heroes are out in the middle of an extremely hostile environment where at any moment they could get chomped, crushed, etc.   Yet Grant stops for a biology lesson.   Get moving, man!   You can talk while you walk, cain'tcha?

-1:33:00 They decide to shut down the system, and only one of these yahoos has the foresight to grab a flashlight.   These guys deserve to be dinosaur food

-1:33:49 "Where are the breakers?"   "Maintenance shed, other end of the compound."   Whose bright idea was that?   These guys deserve to be--wait, I already said that

-1:34:27 Tim's pretty good with his dinosaur knowledge--I was all into dinos when I was his age, but I couldn't have pulled Gallimimus out of my ear

-1:35:35 "Bet you never look at birds the same way again." So even the T-Rex evolved into a bird? Which one? Big Bird?

-1:36:47 There's so little space in here that Hammond has to open the blueprints on Malcolm's <u>broken leg</u>? Sheesh

-1:37:32 I didn't see any headsets sitting with the radios--where's she pick that up?

-1:37:49 PVP problem--it shouldn't take Gennaro and Ellie ten whole seconds to see the raptor fence damage

-1:38:17 It's become vital to get the fences back online. What about our heroes out in the park? What if turning on the fences keeps them locked <u>in</u>? Has nobody thought about that?

-1:39:01 Continuity--Ellie does her little trapeze swing twice

-1:40:06 Grant tosses a stick against the electric wires, and since the stick doesn't, well, burn or start fizzing or anything, he figures they're okay. What did he think would happen? (Note from 2017 review: I still don't think anything would happen, but kind souls have shown me YouTube videos of people hitting high-voltage fences with sticks and bad things DID happen. So (a) I may well be wrong and (b) DON'T THROW ANYTHING AT HIGH-VOLTAGE FENCES)

-1:40:39 Continuity--kids switch places between shots

-1:41:42 Huh--the camera guy goes through a hole in the fence to get that shot--why didn't our heroes crawl through that? (wink, wink)

-1:42:40 Lucky for Tim the slot marked Perimeter Fence was waaaay at the bottom of the list Ellie is going down!   If it was at the top (which would seem to make sense) his arms would still have been through the fence, and he couldn't have been blown off! (which I still have problems with, see below)

-1:42:53 Also lucky for Tim that Ellie takes her <u>sweet</u> time turning on all the systems!

-1:43:25 I've never been electrocuted (I swear) but I've heard stories, and all the stories I've heard involve someone having to knock the chargee away from the wires they've grabbed.   So it's pretty fortunate that Tim was knocked off the fence, and Grant didn't have to go find a long branch. ("Hang on, Tim--well, I guess that's not a problem, ha ha!")

-1:43:26 Continuity! Tim falls straight back, then next shot Grant he's sideways to Grant can catch him

-1:43:45 Nice of the raptor to wait until Ellie was finished with her task before attacking, huh?

-1:43:53 Continuity, Ellie scrabbling at the gate behind her. But <u>fabulous</u> job of acting scared spitless! Continuity on the next shot too

-1:44:06 Arnold's arm was just <u>hanging</u> there? Waiting to be dramatic? (Maybe I'm sick but for some reason this moment made me laugh out loud.) Well, at least he gave Ellie a hand in the end, huh? I'll stop. R.I.P., Mr. Arnold

-1:44:10 Never thought about this before, but this huge perimeter fence...is this the same fence that goes past the Tyrannosaur paddock? Seems like it should be, it's the fence Grant and kids have been dealing with. How can the power come back on past the huge gap Rexy tore in the fence last night? The electrons dribbling out of the fence onto the ground, running over to the other side and jumping into the broken pieces?

-1:45:26 Continuity, raptor attacking Muldoon. R.I.P., dude

-1:46:01 Timmy sure is a trooper.   He has third-degree burns on his hands, abrasions, possible broken bones, anything the current arced through internally (like his heart, lungs, kidneys, etc.) could be <u>burned</u>...but he just trots right along!   (I have the damage estimate on good authority from my friend Janet the E.M.T.)

-1:46:59 The food on the tables--that's been sitting out since at least last night, in the open, yet no flies?   They must use a <u>ton</u> of artificial preservatives on this island! (Which is more dangerous, the dinosaurs or eating the food?)

-1:48:15 The raptor breath blowing on the kitchen window scared the patooties out of me in the theater

-1:49:01 Continuity, raptor coming in the door. And one of these two is the one that just ate Muldoon, right? Sure are careful and neat animals, there's no blood to be seen (I have a vision of a raptor wearing a bib)

-1:49:53 This whole scene in the kitchen still freaks me out, though I'm well aware the kids get away safe. Kudos to the film-makers!

-1:49:55 Didn't Grant say those raptor claws are retractable?   Maybe he didn't know what he's talking about, because it sure doesn't look so

-1:51:18 Lex is in the shelf-thing, trying to lower the door, and the raptor runs into the reflection of her doing so. Lucky (a) the raptor didn't take her time and figure out what the deal was, and (b) lucky that reflection even worked! I think they fudged the angle a bit

`   -1:51:34 Muldoon said the raptors can move at cheetah speed. Fortunately for Gimpy the Human Toast, this particular raptor decides to follow him much more slowly

-1:53:21 "I can't get it unless I move!" Grant and Ellie holding the door. She's holding the hinge side--it's not like she's providing a whole lot of leverage there

-1:53:32 These velociraptors are seriously limber! She's got her face at the window, and yet both hands through the door?

-1:54:28 Hammond asks about his children. Grant: "The children are fine." Sure, don't tell Grand-dad that Timmy needs a doctor as soon as possible. Big liar

-1:55:02 It's a super-great shot, very clever, that the DNA sequencing code is projected onto the side of the velociraptor evil science has created. But...where is this projection coming from?

-1:55:09 Lucky our heroes could just crawl along the ceiling tiles--they usually don't support much weight

-1:55:19 Lex falls through the floor, and looks up before they pull her back in.   Watch the special features--it wasn't Ariana Richards in this shot, it was her stunt double. But much like they did in <u>Titanic</u>, they <u>digitally replaced</u> the stuntwoman's face with Richards!   Since stuntpeople already didn't get enough credit, now we'll erase them altogether!   This makes me mad   (And my apologies to the poor stuntwoman whom I can't even credit by name--I looked all <u>over</u> Al Gore's Internet and couldn't find anyone who knew your name)

-1:55:32 Lucky the vents in this place are human-sized, eh?

-1:56:09 Continuity, Ellie on the T-rex bones.   When the skeleton broke, she started spinning to the left.   Shot changes and suddenly she's spinning right

-1:56:25 Freeze frame here, and you'll get a shot of Richard's stunt-double's face that <u>wasn't</u> replaced, probably because it goes by so fast.   Interesting, though--the shot before this, she let go of her bones and was about to fall to the floor.   Suddenly she's hanging on again

-1:57:06 Runner up for the Will Award!   Yay!   The T-Rex saves the day!!   Well... (A) where did she come from? I thought the fence was up and last we heard T-rex roaring it was on the other side.   (B)   How did she get into the building? (C) How come nobody noticed her until this moment? Ninja Tyrannosaur! (D) Sure is lucky she showed up <u>just</u> in time, huh? (E) Sure is lucky she goes after the raptor and not our heroes, huh? (F) Sure is lucky the <u>other</u> raptor goes after <u>her</u> and not our heroes, huh?

-1:57:38 "After careful consideration, I've decided not to endorse your park." Seriously? After the past twenty-four hours, you're going to get all pithy and sarcastic?

-1:57:50 Surprisingly little blood on the raptor as Rexy shakes it

-1:58:19 Not a nit, necessarily, but interesting--look at the <u>dents</u> on the helicopter door panel? What's up with those?

-1:58:30 Hammond takes a moment to gaze in sorrow at the island which has turned on him. I suppose if Grant had mentioned that his very own grandson needs a hospital, he might step a bit more quickly

-1:59:27 Again, I've never noticed this before. But Grant has the kids in his arms, and the tree canopy goes by the window behind him. Mere feet away. He looks out the other window, and the shot cuts to birds on the open ocean! It's not a jump-cut, because we cut back to him afterwards, and the trees behind him are still there!

Are they still on the island, or over the ocean?   It can't be both!

#15: Harry Potter and the Goblet of Fire

Ruminations: another Harry Potter movie.   Boy, this one sure left out a lot of the book!   Despite being way over two hours long!   No Quidditch World Cup, no shots of the first three competitors fighting the dragons, no Sphinx in the maze.

Do yourself a favor and pick up the book for the real experience...

-0:01:47 Continuity--caretaker turns away from his kitchen window twice

-0:03:18 This caretaker is quite a guy--a gigantic snake just slithered past, and he jerked at the sight but made no sound!

-0:04:00 Yay, a Harry Potter story that doesn't start at the Dursleys!

-0:04:01 Continuity, sleeping Ron (major body movement between wide shot and closeup)

-0:05:22 How do the magical folks keep Muggles from tossing their nasty Port Key objects in the nearest trash can?

-0:06:23 Does juggling with magic really require skill? Is it just a spell that lets the guy in red juggle a jillion swirly things?

-0:07:32 How do they hide this Superbowl sized event from Muggle eyes?   (Like overhead satellites?)

-0:07:55 Continuity--Draco reacts to his father's poke in the gut twice

-0:09:10 Sure is a good trick to get the whole crowd to display Krum posters like that--is everybody in the top half of the stadium supporting Bulgaria?

-0:10:07 Continuity--banner thrown over Ron

-0:11:18 This whole crowd is magical, Muggles not allowed--presumably they all have wands, all have magic training.   Why are the Deatheaters unopposed?

-0:11:27 Sure is lucky Harry doesn't get trampled on, out cold on the ground in a mob like that

-0:13:33 When one is apparating, as the ministry officials did a moment ago, doesn't one have to visualize where they want to end up?   Isn't it seriously dangerous to apparate to a place recently changed, like this burned campground?

-0:14:20 Cho: "Two pumpkin pasties please?"   She's got two friends with her--which one is going to be left out? (I know, I really need to find something better to do)

-0:15:15 Though we know how good Sirius is, he's still a wanted fugitive.   What possible sense does it make to address an envelope to him by name?   If Hedwig or the envelope is intercepted, they'll know it's mail for him...

-0:15:42 The contestants are already arriving--we didn't get to see any of the Quidditch World Cup--they're really trucking along in this film, aren't they?   Maybe this one shoulda been split into two parts like Book 7

-0:15:50 Sure, it's all magical, but that looks like a really uncomfortable ride

-0:16:00 Hagrid's out there playing air-traffic controller?   Really?

-0:16:04 "There's something you don't see every day!"   And they proceed to <u>not</u> show us what George (or Fred) is talking about.   Have a feeling there's going to be a <u>lot</u> of telling-not-showing in this one, people

-0:16:33 The Bulgarian ship surfaces, and starts shedding water.   So it wasn't somehow magically waterproofed, submarine-style, when it was underwater? How did the occupants survive the trip?

-0:19:44 Continuity--Professor Binns, after Hagrid stabs him with the fork

-0:20:10 "Eternal glory" awaits the winner of the Tri-Wizard Tournament.   I dunno, eternity's a long time...

-0:20:48 Huh?   What did Mad-Eye Moody just do? The Hogwarts ceiling just looks like the outside weather...did someone cast a spell?   Is he just playing around, pretending to make the weather better?   I'm very confused

-0:21:30 We'll learn much later that Mad-Eye is an impostor--one would think, as relatively simple as it is to become an exact double for someone else, that there would be security measures to determine who everyone really is

-0:23:20 Again, remembering that Moody is an impostor, the kid playing him is doing a <u>great</u> job on the voice! When Ron and Harry polyjuiced Crabbe and Goyle a coupla movies ago, their voices stayed the same

-0:24:10 I'm going to give out the Will Award fairly early--the assumption that somebody could impersonate an Auror, doing the polyjuice potion thing at least once an hour, for weeks on end--teaching class, interacting with people who know the real guy very well--and all without getting caught? Too implausible for words. Not buying

-0:25:24 Seems odd that anybody in class is laughing as the nasty spider-thing is bounced from face to face...any of them could be next

-0:27:05 Figure Moody is lucky the spider-thing doesn't bite him, picking it up right after using the Cruciartus curse on it

-0:27:51 Didn't polyjuice come with a nasty smell? Moody drinks his right near Harry and Hermione--surprised they have no idea about the stuff

-0:29:15 Where was Cedric Diggory the past three years we've been around Hogwarts? I'm pretty sure I would have noticed this kid...

-0:32:55 Aw, the other champions don't stand a chance, trying to beat Edward Cullen (wink, wink)

-0:33:47 How'd the cup know to dramatically leave Potter's name for last?   (And shouldn't there be <u>some</u> way to absolve Potter from the competition?   He didn't put his name in, he's not old enough, etc. etc...)

-0:34:12 ...and Ron's already mad that Harry's name came out of the cup.   Five seconds after it did.   That didn't take long!   (Everything's been speeded up to get us through this one!)

-0:34:43 When Fred and George thought they got their names in the cup, everybody cheered--why all the angst now?

-0:35:26 "Did you put your name in?"   "No sir." "Did you ask one of the older students to do it for you?"   So <u>that</u> would've worked?   When ageing potion didn't?   I'm surprised nobody tried that...

-0:36:00 "The Goblet of Fire constitutes a binding magical contract."   Even when the "signature" is invalid? Seems fishy

-0:37:50 Dumbledore pulls out a memory and puts it in his little vase.   Does he no longer have any recollection of the event, then?   Or is it a copying-type situation, convenient for showing Harry the more important stuff later?

-0:39:49 Continuity, Rita Skeeter as shot changes

-0:40:12 Rita knows Harry lived in a broom cupboard? How? And is anybody else bothered by an adult and a child all alone in this sort of situation?

-0:41:26 How can Harry possibly read the notepad that's turned away from him (and a magical quill writing in cursive, no less?)

-0:41:52 An owl comes into the owlery and Harry is waiting for his post. How'd he know it was coming then--or has he just been up here for hours? How'd he know the owl that just came in was for him--especially since Sirius says he couldn't send Hedwig? And how does the owl know not to deliver Harry's post to the breakfast table like every other bit of mail?

-0:43:01 So the newspaper was reading Skeeter's column out loud? Where has that effect been in every other paper we've seen in this world?

-0:44:00 The Gary Oldman fire effect is really very well done

-0:45:50 Seeing as how Moody is a fake, why is he being so nice to Neville? (Not that I mind, about time somebody gave that kid some respect)

-0:46:00 Seriously?   Hermione has to go through all the names of people instead of just saying "Hagrid's looking for you?"   Why is she letting Ron do this to her?

-0:47:36 Invisibility cloak effect continues to be just incredibly well done

-0:47:50 Harry's sticking his tongue out at the thought of Hagrid in love--what is this kid, seven?

-0:48:33 So how hard was it to get a fourth dragon in here for the unexpected competitor?   That must've been a logistical nightmare

-0:49:02 The second shot of the fire-breathing horntail looks exactly the same as the first

-0:49:43 Does Cedric have rouge on?   I suppose he's allowed, but...

-0:50:30 I really don't think Draco would be in a tree. I expect him to give Harry a hard time, be a jerk--but he's sitting in a tree?   Who thought that would make sense?

-0:50:38 Continuity--Harry stalks right up to Draco, shot changes and he has to walk up again

-0:52:44 Fake Moody explains his Foe Glass.   Does the Foe Glass work for Fake Moody, or is it trying to register for the real one locked in the trunk?

-0:53:51 Moody's trying to get Potter to come up with a dragon-defeating plan.   How can the boy, when he has no idea what he's going to be expected to do?   A plan to get, say, past the dragon (or grab an egg) would be far different from a plan to, say, <u>kill</u> said dragon...

-0:54:21 Fred and George are allowed to play bookie at the Tri-Wizard Tournament?   Really?

-0:56:34 Continuity, Potter and Crouch as shot changes

-0:57:17 The dragon-dealing rules said nothing about a time limit.   So why not wait until your dragon falls asleep, hmmm?

-0:57:34 Sorry, you don't get to see the others fight the dragons.   Too bad for you

-0:58:15 Continuity as dragon tosses Harry around

-0:58:25 There's nothing keeping the dragon from flaming the spectators--seems dangerous

-0:59:30 The Firebolt was on it's way, was just about two seconds out, and then Harry ducked behind a boulder for awhile.   How'd the broomstick know to go around in a holding pattern and wait for him to peek out again?

-1:00:41 For all the stuff in the book we haven't seen, this dragon chase around Hogwarts <u>wasn't</u> in the book

-1:00:55 Continuity as Harry falls (in several successive shots, as well)

-1:01:06 Why is the dragon clawing his way around the tower, instead of <u>flying</u> after his meal?

-1:06:52 Is there a reason why the bell on the Hogwarts Victrola needs to be big as all outdoors?

-1:09:56 By the age of six Hagrid could pick up his own father?   If the man was that small compared to momma, one wonders how Hagrid was created.   Not that I'm asking for details

-1:10:01 Did the large woman just eat something she found in Hagrid's beard?   Seriously?   Eeeeugh

-1:11:29 Continuity after Snape whacks Harry with the book

-1:12:33 Continuity, Cho and Harry in the doorway

-1:22:32 Somebody's been busy--all the dragon claw damage on the towers seems to be fixed

-1:22:46 Continuity, the crow going up to Harry's window.

-1:24:00 Good to see Neville win one for once

-1:25:55 Cedric sure doesn't have much faith in Harry--he just gives him a clue about the egg, without asking if he's cracked it yet

-1:26:04 How'd Harry get into the Prefect's bathroom again?

-1:26:06 And...what do the Prefects need with a 30 person Jacuzzi?

-1:26:18 Nice of the stained-glass moving mermaid to respect the PG-13 rating and <u>just</u> keep those things covered

-1:28:08 When Harry surfaces after listening to the egg's message, the opened egg pops out of the water--but no scream?

-1:28:32 Anybody else find it creepy that the ghost is trying to get a glimpse of Harry's...fiddly bits?   It was creepy in the book, it's worse in the movie.   I liked her better whiny than seductive

-1:29:14 New library policy that has books flying about?   This didn't happen in previous three movies

-1:30:30 What are the odds--the ghillieweed will work for an hour (more or less) and Harry needs it to work for an hour!

-1:32:33 Sure is bright down here at the bottom of the Black Lake

-1:32:49 The ghillieweed gave Potter fins and gills, everything he'll need--but didn't put eyes on either side of his head, or force a dorsal fin on him, or anything--convenient stuff!

-1:34:27 Four people tethered underwater, looking drowned...I question the PG-13 rating here

-1:35:28 I'm surprised half-shark-half-Krum can still function--and lucky for Hermione he ain't too hungry, huh?

-1:39:00 Dumbledore ain't holding the wand against his throat anymore--how is he still amplified?   That's not how it worked for Fudge earlier

-1:43:30 A weird, glowing object just moved forward out of concealment in Dumbledore's office.   And rather than respecting Big D's privacy and moving away from it, Harry is all over it, waving his wand and poking his nose.   For shame!

-1:44:08 Lucky that Potter got a memory he needed to move the plot along, and not some random lunch date of Dumbledore's, huh?

-1:51:00 Fleur totally botched the Lake task--how come she gets to keep playing?

-1:51:10 Sheesh, could we have at least a moment of silence for Barty Crouch?   No?   Tournament goes on as scheduled as though he hadn't been killed?   Well...okay

-1:57:26 So the only way to get Harry to Voldemort-- which was the whole point of Fake Moody putting Harry's name into the Goblet of Fire--is because the Tri-Wizard Cup is a Port Key.   (Get all that?   Maybe we should go to the flowchart for this)   It's a pretty haphazard plan of Tom Riddle's, relying as it does on Harry not getting killed by the dragon, drowning in the lake, dying in the maze...

-1:57:54 By the way, if you saw the movie and didn't read the book--always read the book.   Always.   But especially this time, as roughly 90% of what happened in the maze in the book is <u>not</u> shown on screen.   You don't see the Sphinx, the giant spider...

...second thought, the movie's just fine

-1:59:22 Here's a problem: in the books when one grabs a Port Key, one is along for the ride until they get to the Key's destination.   There's no "letting go" mid-journey, or late in the journey to ensure a safe (if dorky) landing like we saw way back at the beginning of the movie.   But with the filmmakers changing the rules, and making it possible to let go of a Key, <u>why</u> don't Harry and Cedric let go once they realize they're going for a ride?   Why trust where this unexpected Key is taking them?

-2:00:10 And suddenly it's for real, as someone we care about dies!   RIP, Edward

-2:00:30 Is Wormtail horked at Voldemort or something?   Sure, he has to put Big Bad into the cauldron, but it seems very disrespectful for Wormy to dump Voldy in from five feet up like that

-2:00:58 ...and Wormtail cuts off his own hand. We're really pushing the PG-13 rating here, MPAA...

-2:01:15 Lucky for Harry that all they needed was a drop or two of blood, and not a hand or foot or something, huh?

-2:01:45 Do very much appreciate the filmmakers not showing us Voldemort's junk.   Nice of the magical transformation to provide him with black, flowy robes, too

-2:02:10 I bet Ralph Fiennes, the actor who plays Voldy, just <u>loves</u> trying to breathe through those little slits

-2:03:14 Considering that his life is in mortal danger, I think Harry could be struggling quite a bit more with that statue--and I'm pretty sure if he <u>really</u> wanted to he could get free

-2:03:23 The Dark Mark went up about ten seconds ago, and right away people start apparating in wearing Deatheater costumes!   They just hanging around wearing those all the time?

-2:03:40 "Thirteen years it's been."   Waitaminute. Potter got his scar, which backfired and cursed Voldemort, when our hero was a baby.   Our hero is now <u>fourteen</u>.   I think Voldy's math is off somewhere.

-2:03:57 Continuity--Voldemort dumps Goyle on his butt, turns past a shrinking female Deatheater--shot changes and the female is suddenly kneeling

-2:04:49 Continuity, Voldy's wand as he heals Wormtail

-2:05:18 Continuity--Harry's chin is on the stone scythe, shot changes and his chin jumps several inches

-2:06:09 Voldemort is free to touch Harry now! And yet somehow Harry gets out of here alive!   Did I already give out the Will Award?   I did.   Oh, well

-2:06:53 Continuity as Voldy attacks Harry

-2:08:23 Continuity--just as Harry puts both hands on his wand, the shot changes and he's one-handing it again

-2:08:42 Second time lucky--Harry didn't die the first time because of his mother's love, and he doesn't die here because his and Voldy's wands are so evenly matched. Wonder what will magically show up to save his tush next movie?   (I just checked--Dumbledore.   Good luck with that in movie eight, Harry)

-2:09:18 The spirits of Harry's parents were in Voldy's wand?   I didn't get this in the book and it's no clearer now.   Lucky his dad can talk, though, and has the info Harry needs

-2:09:45 All Harry says is "Ascio" and the Port Key flies towards him.   I thought he had to say the name of what he wanted?   As in "Ascio Firebolt?"

-2:14:15 ?!?   Is Fake Moody flipping Harry off right here?

-2:15:06 Continuity--Fake Moody smacks into the wall twice.   And how lucky Dumbledore showed up just in time, huh?

-2:16:30 How did Fake Moody get real Moody's magical eye to do his bidding?

-2:16:45 Gasp!   It's not Mad-Eye Moody, it's Doctor Who!   (wink, wink)

-2:17:15 How did Moody get out of Azkaban?   (I swear, that place is just a revolving door)

-2:21:16 Ah, good old Hogwarts. Almost completely white faces, and not a handicapped person in sight

#16: Ice Age 3

Ruminations: Why, oh why, didn't I take the it's-my-book-I'll-change-things-if-I-want-to initiative and nitpick The Chronicles of Narnia instead of this? Grr.

Anyway, if the shoe fits, shame on you! I don't own Ice Age 3, so borrowed such from the public library. And I wasn't seventeen seconds into the film before the disk started skipping! If you are going to borrow something that isn't yours, could you try and return it without damage? Or do I ask too much?

While I'm on the subject, stop throwing your trash on the ground.   Find a doggone dumpster already!

-0:00:43 I thought Scrat ended up frozen in an ice cube and thawed in modern times?   Why is he back here in the Ice Age?

-0:01:29 Just how do they make a squirrel look sexy? Or—better question—where does a squirrel get eyeshadow and long lashes?

-0:02:55 So Scrat's little sparring partner is a flying squirrel?   Why did she fall for ages before putting this ability to work?

-0:03:09 With that kind of fall, Scrat's gotta be dead

-0:03:39 Why does a mammoth mamma need boiling water to give birth?

-0:04:47 Sid asks a women when she's due and she's not pregnant.   Comedian Brian Regan says the rule of thumb for guessing if a woman is preggo is "Never, ever, ever." And I can say from first-hand experience, guessing and being wrong is not a fun feeling!

-0:05:12 Why does the deer have a horn on his nose?   Why does that prove it's a prehistoric deer?

-0:06:29 Why do mammoths, even baby ones, need a playground?

-0:06:54 With what delicate appendages did Manny fashion that mobile?   His trunk?

-0:12:06 Why did T-Rex leave her eggs...and in a <u>cold</u> environment?   Wouldn't that be harmful to them?

-0:12:15 Where did Sid get the crayon to draw his egg's faces?

-0:13:20 Those eggs roll awfully straight, considering they're egg-shaped

-0:14:10 Lucky Sid and the eggs fly through the air in slo-motion, huh?

-0:14:26 And Ellie's at the bottom of the hill?   So Sid climbed this hill for a day, to get away from the mammoths that rejected him, before he found the eggs???

-0:15:15 They have popsicles here?

-0:17:00 How did the eggs not get, well, scrambled by that hill roll?   Imagine a woman eight months pregnant in a somersault contest

-0:18:30 Lucky for Sid the newly hatched dinosaurs thought "mama" and not "lunch"!

-0:18:48 How do fish scream? Especially underwater?

-0:20:20 The elusive Scrat-focused acorn pops up in a <u>bubble</u>? Really?

-0:20:33 Both Scrat and the sultry squirrel are running in their respective bubbles—why does she go up while he goes down?

-0:21:28 Why don't the animals act like animals? One little gate keeps everybody out of the playground?

-0:22:13 "I'm a single mother with three kids." Sid doesn't even know his own <u>sex</u>?

-0:22:30 Sure, the little Rexes are causing mayhem at the playground, but as far as I can tell, they <u>still</u> haven't eaten. Since birth, I mean. So it could be much worse

-0:25:20 Time for the Will Award! Amazing to me that underneath all this Ice Age stuff is a prehistoric Jurassic Park that <u>nobody</u> up on the surface knew about. How this environment even <u>exists</u> is another question

-0:27:00 Guess it makes sense that Mama Rex understands English?

-0:31:05 Lucky our heroes weren't killed by the ankylosaurus. I'm thankful for this review if for no other reason than I get to use the word <u>ankylosaurus</u>

-0:31:28 "Yabba Dabba Doo!" The mammoth's heard of the Flintstones?

-0:32:25 How did Buck make two mammoths and a saber-toothed tiger just disappear?

-0:36:02 "Abandon all hope, ye who enter here." They've heard of Dante's <u>Inferno</u>?

-0:37:38 Plants have eyeballs? Since when?

-0:38:48 Manny and Diego trapped in a plant. Claws, tusks, no effect? It's a <u>plant</u>!

-0:42:06 T-Rex snot disappears when shot changes. Not that I'm complaining

-0:42:18 Point of View as Sid drops—there's nothing below him but ground. Shot changes and he's tangled in vines! Where'd those come from?

-0:43:42 Really? A cell-phone rock?

-0:44:56 Really? A cable car made out of a dinosaur skeleton? Who put <u>that</u> in place?

-0:46:05 Really? An <u>Alvin and the Chipmunks</u> CHRISTMAS song?

-0:47:04 How did T-Rex and company get past the big, gassy cavern?

-0:47:51 Ellie's mad at Manny. Why? For getting stuck? For having to breathe? The gas deal sure wasn't his fault. Females…

-0:50:10 The kids toss the empty bone into shot. Boy, they sure ate quietly

-0:52:09 Why would giant huge-o-saurus Rudy even notice, much less bother with, little Buck the weasel?

-0:52:55 Dinosaurs have uvulas? I had no idea. Also the perspective is a bit off—Buck should be smaller than any of Rudy's teeth, certainly not big enough to hang on the uvula

-0:53:04 "Back and forth and back…and forth" while Buck is pantomiming his uvula battle, please notice that he's in mid-air, hanging on to…<u>nothing</u>

-0:53:18 So to make a knife of the proper size, Buck apparently snagged one of Rudy's baby teeth. Cause all the others are way too big—and differently shaped to boot

-0:57:07 How'd Scrat get off the tar-soaked tree?

-1:01:05 Didn't we do the precariously balanced rock scene in the <u>last</u> Ice Age movie?

-1:03:29 Manny runs past Diego, shot changes, and he runs past Diego again

-1:06:01 I also didn't know it was possible to rope a pterodactyl just like a horse! (I do so love the word pterodactyl tho)

-1:09:30 Passing pterodactyls make a buzzing noise, almost as if they had engines—which they don't

-1:10:20 Really? They had altimeters, and C.P.R., and "Mayday" calls back in prehistoric times?

-1:10:48 How does the pterodactyl glide <u>up</u> the falls?

-1:12:02 Really? They had Lamaze back in...okay, I'll stop

-1:12:20 Huh? Baby woolly mammoths sound <u>just</u> like baby humans!

-1:12:23 But fortunately for the sensitive-stomached, baby woolly mammoths do not come with afterbirth of any kind

-1:13:17 I haven't thought about this until now, through all three movies, but...how does Diego talk so clearly with those tusks?

-1:16:18 How'd the party get back up past the gassy chasm?

-1:18:00 Nice that conveniently long vines are just everywhere, now that we need to drop a giant dinosaur in his tracks

-1:24:24 Well, if one can ride a pterodactyl like a horse, I guess one can ride a huge-o-saurus like a horse...

-1:24:40 Really?   Squirrels make their mates move furniture?

Ow!   Okay, I'm done.   I swear.   Stop pinching me

#17: Spider-Man 3

Ruminations: despite crying, jazz piano, etc., I really enjoyed this movie.   And the Venom effects are really well done!

-0:03:23 Spidey is swinging by on a New York big-board.   Who is taking these mid-air swing-by shots?

-0:03:27 Continuity, kids next to Peter

-0:06:52 Continuity as Peter chases Harry.   As shot changes, gal behind them with flowers disappears

-0:08:08 The Hobgoblin (I know he's called the New Goblin in the credits, but I'm a comic book fan, and the son of Norman Osborn who fights Spider-Man is the Hogboglin. Deal with it) prepares for battle.   So Harry can just make all these cool gadgets?   Flying snowboard, etc.?

-0:08:30 So Harry took a dose of goblin juice too? Why didn't he go crazy like his old man?

-0:08:40 Aw, Peter and MJ on a date in central park. And since Peter doesn't give a fig for his secret identity, he's made a giant web for them to lie on.   How sticky and gross and romantic!

-0:08:43 Continuity.   As the shot changes, Pete and MJ are much closer

-0:09:44 Interesting that Peter's spider sense, the sense that let him notice the approaching Green Goblin from about a half-mile away in the first movie, fails to notice a meteorite strike about twenty feet behind him.   That sure is some kiss, I guess

-0:10:00 What a coincidence that the alien symbiote would just happen to land near and find Parker!

-0:11:09 Marko eases a window open to sneak into his home.   This is Queens, at night—I do <u>not</u> buy that <u>anybody's</u> window is unlocked

-0:17:49 Harry has created a flying snowboard, and all he can think about is vengeance?   I suppose he's already filthy rich, but still!

-0:17:55 Continuity.   Harry punches the wall, shot changes and he's punching the wall

-0:18:10 How does that piece of wall just keep its shape as Peter falls, still attached to it?   Seems like it would crumble

-0:18:55 If Harry's not attached to the flying snowboard, how does he stay on through all this?   If he <u>is</u> attached somehow, how'd Pete get him off it so easy?

-0:19:00 Wow…the board even flies <u>itself</u>

-0:19:13 Pete, in mid-air, drops the precious engagement ring at 18:45.   He catches it here.   How high up were they that the ring was <u>still</u> falling thirty seconds after he dropped it?

-0:19:16 Parker's suit is amazingly clean and un-ripped considering the battle!

-0:19:50 Harry is brand-new at the supervillain thing. Pete's been swinging around for a year or three.   How does Harry keep up so easy?   --and oh yeah, since <u>when</u> is the Hobgoblin a ninja snowboarder?

-0:20:10 Where do those pumpkin bombs come from, and how is the board powered?   See glider comments, first Spider-Man movie

-0:20:20 Sure is lucky for Pete that Harry wants to toy with him, and throws the bat-wing bombs and not the skeletonizer (maybe those things are <u>really</u> expensive--since it's only used one time in all three movies)

-0:20:44 How do the bat-wing bombs keep flying? What is propelling them?

-0:20:59 Ooh, clothesline!   Harry was flipping backwards after the hit.   Shot changes and he's now flipping <u>forwards</u>

-0:21:40 Peter performs sloppy CPR on Harry.   He better be careful, with that superstrength of his

-0:22:40 Marko being chased by police.   Dog catches up, and goes for his <u>throat</u>.   I've seen police dog training, and dogs are supposed to go for arms or legs, not the throat (maybe it's different in New York)

-0:22:45 What a guy!   Marko just scales a barbed-wire fence like it's no big deal

-0:22:50 Continuity, flashlights between close-up and wide shot

-0:23:24 The scientists, working this delicate and strange experiment: "There's a change in the silicon mass." "Probably a bird."   Considering this delicate and likely expensive test, wouldn't it be nice to eyeball the scene, and make sure of your site?

-0:24:12 So...demolecularization equals turned into sand?

-0:24:19 Seems like this process would be incredibly painful.   Marko is so tough, though, that he pretty much doesn't react at all

-0:24:30 Well, Marko must be dead.   No way he coulda survived that

-0:25:08 How convenient—Harry has short-term amnesia!   Does anybody experience this in real life?

-0:25:48 No residue from the ferocious battle besides the head wound?

-0:27:35 The sand thing is ridiculously implausible, but the effect is really, really good

-0:28:30 It's pretty early in the movie, but nonetheless time for the Will Award!   Which goes to the idea that Marko could even <u>survive</u> this demolecularization, much less gain a super power!

-0:29:01 Why didn't Marko's locket turn to sand like <u>everything</u> else?

-0:29:10 How does he see the locket with sand eyeballs?   How does he make his wavy hair out of sand crystals?

Clothes?   Shoes?   Shoelaces?   Is anybody else finding this a little silly?

-0:30:08 Since he's making his clothes out of sand anyway, couldn't he make nicer ones?

-0:31:59 Peter hears the distress call and changes into Spider-Man...in <u>five</u> seconds!   Amazing spider powers!

-0:32:01 The mask in Pete's hands doesn't look big enough to cover his head...

-0:32:04 ...but now after we cut away and come back, it's attached, so I guess I was wrong

-0:33:11 Out of control girder breaks glass, then breaks the same glass, then breaks <u>the same glass</u>

-0:34:10 That sure is some zoom lens.   Brock can tell from <u>sixty-two stories</u> down (620 feet!) that it's Gwen hanging out the window?!

-0:37:40 It's a nice gag, but this buzzer of Jameson's—who has a buzzer that shakes their whole desk?

-0:39:50 In my Spider-Man 2 review I mentioned how every woman in this version of the Big Apple seems to be a model.   In the commentary, right about here Kirsten Dunst talks about the same thing

-0:39:54 Everybody catch the Stan Lee cameo?   Just checking

-0:40:00 By the way, about that cameo: Lee's final line to Peter Parker is "'Nuff said."   Which he used to say a <u>lot</u> back in the 60s when he was writing pretty much all of the Marvel comics.   Funny—the DVD subtitles have "Enough said" as his line, which would be wrong

-0:40:58 "Looks like I'm not hurting for money." Just how much memory did Harry lose?   "Any girlfriends?" Sheesh

-0:45:13 Cop walks under falling sand, but none seems to reach him.   That's the problem with digital sand, I guess

-0:45:30 Cop tugs on corner of truck cover and the whole thing just <u>whooshes</u> off

-0:46:16 Marko didn't flinch during demolecularization, yet he now is reacting as if the bullets are hurting.   Huh?   How do bullets hurt <u>sand</u>?

-0:46:27 How does Marko even make a sand whirlwind, much less keep it together as he travels around New York?

-0:47:46 Pete swings in—as Peter Parker, he swings in—and stops to get into costume.   This is New York, there are people everywhere.   Does he care nothing for his secret identity?   He's maskless in view of the crowd!   And people with cameras that can zoom sixty stories!

-0:48:15 How does Spidey <u>slow himself down</u> in mid-air for the high-fives?

-0:48:36 Does it make sense for the crowd to immediately, ravenously, start shouting "kiss him!"   These folks need to get out more

-0:50:01 A bit of sand falls on the bank truck accelerator, and the truck speeds up.   A few grains of sand on the pedal, and acceleration??

-0:50:25 Sandman figured out how to shift his molecules and let Spidey's punch go through him <u>awful</u> fast

-0:50:29 Continuity, sand punch

-0:50:30 Continuity.   Spidey goes out the truck's backdoor, and then goes out the truck's backdoor again

-0:50:32 Spidey comes out the back door, falls backward, then in mid-air flips himself <u>forward</u>?   Screw you, laws of physics!

-0:50:47 Diving headfirst, Spidey does a mid-air flip to land feet-first.   See previous comment

-0:51:21 So in one-tenth of a second Spidey can form an entire web?   Nice!

-0:51:35 We see that don't-think-it's-big-enough mask again as Parker reveals his face

-0:51:48 Continuity, Pete's head during sand spit

-1:00:31 Marko threatening Uncle Ben.   Gun comes up in closeup, change to wide, gun comes up again

-1:00:35 Marko must really love that shirt.   He's making it out of sand now, he was wearing it during the demolecularization—and he had it on the night he shot Uncle Ben!   (And took his rice!)

-1:03:54 What does the symbiote use for eyes, to see where it wants to go??

-1:04:57 How does this alien stuff make itself into a cool costume?

-1:05:47 Nice of the symbiote to let Pete take the mask off, since he's basically ripping the alien apart to do so

-1:06:53 The black costume is in a trunk.   So...Pete had the black costume over his Spidey outfit, it let go, and reformed into a costume all by itself?   Which Pete then decided to keep??

-1:07:03 Falling headfirst, then flips around in mid-air to put his feet down.   Nuh-uh, Spidey

-1:09:04 Every action has an equal and opposite reaction.   It's a law of physics, take it up with Newton.   So when Spidey swings in at Sandman, and the Sandman stops him with a kick, Marko should be rocked back.   But he ain't.

-1:09:21 Sandman makes teeth out of sand too? (And lungs?   And vocal cords?)

-1:10:04 Continuity, Spidey

-1:10:18 Continuity, water!   Spidey releases the boiler (or tank, or whatever this is) and the first shot has the water reach Sandman CUT the water is 20 feet away, then reaches Sandman CUT the water's 5 feet away, washes over him CUT water hits him again CUT the water hits him a third time and finally washes the guy away (sheesh)

-1:11:08 Three seconds ago Pete passed his landlord's closed door.   Now suddenly it's open, and Ursula is there, all without sound.   Ninja neighbor!

-1:17:14 Continuity.   MJ reaches for something, CUT her hands are on the table

-1:17:34 Continuity as the cute couple does the twist

-1:23:06 So instead of MJ telling Pete "Harry's gone crazy, he threatened me," she breaks up with him.   She sure don't trust the Spidey skills

-1:26:20 Pete leaves the café, looks back at Harry who winks at him, then the bus passes between the two— and Harry's gone?   Did he disapparate?

-1:27:10 Now Pete's the one with the invisibility cloak, suddenly appearing at Harry's

-1:27:29 Huh.   The symbiote brings out a person's inner Emo?

-1:27:47 Continuity.   Pete punches Harry, the shot changes and he re-punches Harry

-1:32:48 Continuity.   Pete's got the phone at his right ear CUT his left ear CUT away from his head

-1:33:17 It only takes six seconds for Ursula to get Pete his milk?!

-1:35:00 Oy.   Dancing Parker.   Let's move on…

-1:35:35 How in the name of all that is Marvel did the Sandman survive that wash down the sewer?

-1:35:38 And he still has the locket!

-1:37:28 Oy.   The symbiote taught Pete how to play jazz piano?   And be a jerk?

-1:38:08 What about Pete taking his jacket off suddenly makes it physically possible for Gwen's hair to blow back?

-1:40:34 Continuity, MJ's arm

-1:41:43 Eight zillion people in New York, what are the odds that Brock would wander right by Pete fighting with the symbiote?

-1:43:32 Pete fighting the symbiote is very, very well done

-1:47:08 Aunt May came all the way over to see Peter—and after three minutes she's ready to go.   These New Yorkers, no staying power

-1:47:52 The symbiote goes so far as to make scary teeth, even!

-1:48:07 Why is Venom doing spider-like things, crawling on walls and such?   Brock doesn't have spider-powers…

-1:48:59 MJ gets into cab and…it's Eddie!   Where did Eddie get a cab from, one might ask, or how did he know where MJ lived or when she would come out?

-1:49:48 Again with the excellent camerawork—this newsguy is zooming in on MJ from about 80 stories down!

-1:50:00 Peter slooowly opens his Spidey-suit case. Chop chop, dude!   This is no time for drama!

-1:51:55 Jarvis the butler, to Harry: "The night your father died, I cleaned his wound."   <u>Jarvis</u> took care of the dead Green Goblin?   What were the police up to that night?

-1:53:12 Continuity, as car falls into webbing

-1:55:47 Takes MJ almost twenty-three seconds to almost hit the ground.   She sure falls slow

-1:56:23 See, the dump truck falls from the same height and hits in 4 seconds!

-1:56:33 Assuming we believe Sandman capable of forming himself into a giant, where does he get the stamina to power this huge form?

-1:57:20 I doubt the physics work, the ones that have Spidey pulling himself up sixty stories in mid-air

-1:58:40 Spidey getting a beat-down and the police just stand there?

-1:59:00 Harry loses his Hobgoblin mask without using his hands—where's the button for <u>that</u>?

-1:59:42 Of course the ninja hoversnowboard has a <u>flamethrower</u>

-2:00:16 Little sassy girl with the camera sells it to Jameson, then—ha, ha—there's no film inside.   So what was the kid doing taking pics a moment ago?   Practicing?

-2:01:00 Another one of them slo-motion falls

-2:02:08 Does giant Sandman feel pain?   Why? Regular sand don't

-2:05:39 Nice of the explosion to completely wipe away all traces of Venom and Eddie Brock.   Bits left lying around would be pretty gross, I figger

-2:07:30 Uncle Ben was shot by accident!   Kids— don't mess around with guns!   Anyway, after this big reveal, Pete can forgive Marko for Uncle Ben's death, and we're supposed to feel Marko is no longer a bad guy.   Shame about all those dead and injured cops down there, though...

-2:08:03 Pete shares his pain with Marko.   "I've done terrible things too."   Yeah, like that whole jazz piano scene

-2:09:08 How does Sandman hold on to that locket when he's in whirlwind mode?

-2:09:15 Pete needs to reexamine his priorities.   His new best friend Harry is seriously injured, but he takes time out for Sandman talk instead of swinging to nearest hospital!

-2:10:54 The sun is coming up?   Twenty minutes after the battle ended?   What was that sassy little girl doing out at 4 a.m.??

#18: Shrek 2

Ruminations: It's not often that a sequel tops the original.   I can think of only one other example right off my head--Terminator II.   I am told that the second Shrek movie made more money in its opening weekend than the first did its entire theatrical run.   I don't really think the sequel is a hundred times better than the original, and something of the first's love story was a little lost--but it's certainly a fun ride.

So let's get started!   Oh, right after I feel sorry for that kid up there in the moon.   He's been fishing for, what, eighteen years now?   Is he ever gonna catch anything?

-0:00:01 Because it's a kids movie, and for comedy, there are a lot of modern items that don't fit in a medieval setting.   And I wouldn't have it any other way, but this is a nitpicker's guide.   Rather than make a noting every moment kind of listing, I'm going to throw down all the ones I noticed right here: videocameras, in-flight movies, Mexican food, buffalo wings, the Crusades, fast food, Shirley Basset, Keebler Elves, Brothers Grimm, Pretty Woman, Annie, Miranda rights, Starbucks, breakdancing, "La Vida Loca", bullets, crowd surfing, Prince Charles, doing the Worm, stage lights, microphones, "All By Myself", "Rawhide", and <u>Footloose</u>.

-0:00:02 Because it's a kids movie, and for comedy...yeah, you already read that part. (Didn't you?) Along with modern references, there are also a number of fun parodies.   Because I'm a list kinda guy, here are the ones I noted: <u>Flashdance</u>, Michael Jackson, Indiana Jones, Lord of the Rings (more than once), E.T., COPS, <u>Mission Impossible</u>, <u>Beauty and the Beast</u>, <u>Alien</u>, Justin Timberlake, <u>Jurassic Park</u>, the Hollywood sign, and The Beatles ("Sergeant Pompous and his Fancy Pants Club Band)

-0:01:30 Sure is lucky for Fiona that Charming was a week late, and Shrek rescued her

-0:01:45 Charming shoots an arrow across the gorge (and it's a really good trick that it caught, and was able to bear his whole weight!), ziplines across with his bow, lands...and the bow has disappeared

-0:02:03 And where was he keeping a <u>spritzer</u> all this time?   That armor have pockets?

-0:02:20 It's a funny callback to the first movie.   But how did the wolf get to the castle, to be in Fiona's old bed? And just 'cause it's a rent-free establishment, is there <u>food</u> enough for a wolf?

-0:03:00 Shrek breaks the door carrying his wife across the threshold--next shot door's all fixed

-0:04:10 While dealing with marauders, Fiona spins upside-down in a tight dress. She can't spread her legs enough to kick the guys surrounding her, but they're nice enough to fall down anyway

-0:09:12 I'd nitpick how Donkey managed to get invited along for the journey to Mom and Dad's, but Donkey pretty much does what he wants, doesn't he?

-0:10:20 The kingdom is called Far, Far Away. Which makes sense initially--does the kingdom next door still call them Far, Far Away, though?

-0:12:50 It's a huge surprise when the Ogres step out of the carriage. The carriage windows have been open this whole time--nobody could see them? (I know I'm not nitpicking the original, but there is a long period in the first Shrek where Fiona doesn't realize our hero is an ogre, just because a helmet is covering half his face! Not his green skin, not his size...)

-0:12:58 Closeup shot, tons of confetti. Cut wide-- confetti gone!

-0:15:51 Mom, Dad, Shrek, Fiona all sitting around the dinner table. There's a fifth chair. Nobody has invited

Donkey--did they all just <u>know</u> he would show up anyway? Why the fifth chair?

-0:15:43 Switcheroo!   The plate with the little weird things on it magically becomes a fingerbowl between frames. Not just in front of Shrek but at every place setting!

-0:16:22 Somehow, to emphasize what a bumpkin Shrek is, even <u>Donkey</u> knows that it's a fingerbowl and not soup.   Really?   Donkey went to charm school?

-0:17:41 Is it likely that Donkey would know that the Queen's name is Lillian?

-0:19:31 This Fairy Godmother must keep busy--if she arrives on-scene every time <u>anybody</u> in the kingdom sheds a tear!   (Or was she just hovering out of sight waiting for Fiona to be unhappy?   And how out of touch is this woman that she doesn't know Fiona has taken a husband?)

-0:23:15 "I've made changes for you, Shrek."   This sentence implies that Fiona being ogre-like instead of human was a conscious choice made out of love for him.   Really? We saw in the first movie that every night she turned into this ogre-like form, and then True Love's Kiss made it permanent. So if she'd kissed Farquaad, or Charming, she would've remained human?   What if she'd kissed a dwarf?   Where's the delineation?

Beyond that, forgetting my original point here--Fiona claims it was a choice she made.   Yet when she stayed ogre-like she seemed as surprised as everyone else, didn't she?

(All of this is making me reconsider the message of the original <u>Shrek</u>.   I felt what they were saying was "Beauty comes from the inside, and real love sees this" which is a fantastic message.   But now, considering how similar in appearance they are, the message kinda seems like "Find someone to love who looks like you," which isn't very good at all

-0:26:28 Fairy Godmother doesn't have to pay for her fast food?

-0:31:00 Ha--Sleeping Beauty is having a slumber party.   Wait, that doesn't make sense

-0:32:36 "7:30 by the old oak."   So...there's only one oak in the forest?

-0:34:24 Puss In Boots leaps forward off Shrek's shoulder, then next shot is spinning sideways like a ninja throwing star

-0:34:57 Did the hairball hacking really have to go on for twenty seconds?

-0:36:45 Further evidence that the Fairy Godmother was hovering around Fiona earlier--our heroine didn't cry on a card, she just cried, which doesn't help the boys

-0:43:10 Fairy Godmother, in her diatribe about "no ogres" in the "happily ever after" stories mentions The Little Mermaid.   Assuming she's talking about the original fairytale...read that one sometime.   It's about the unhappiest ending around

-0:46:30 Repeating crossbows?   Really?   Sure is lucky all three thousand arrows miss, huh?

-0:47:10 Lucky for all that the huge vat contained some version of Happy Ever After juice, and not something evil or deadly.   Considering the whole factory is coated in it

-0:49:00 The Happy Ever After potion makes the ugly look beautiful.   Which is pretty subjective, but anyway--Puss volunteers to take the potion.   What, I wonder, would have happened?   (Would he have turned into a dog?   Just kidding, I'm a cat person, don't send me emails)

-0:51:32 "Hey boss--let's shave him."   With what, exactly?

-0:53:42 "Are you from Europe?"   Aren't   they   in Europe?

-0:57:03 "Tell Princess Fiona her husband, Sir Shrek, is here to see her."   So...the potion not only makes you cute, it also conveys knighthood?

-0:59:16 Fairy Godmother traps Shrek in Fiona's bedroom.   He can see her down on the steps talking to Charming, tries to shout to her but the glass is too thick. Knowing Shrek's temper and love for Fiona, I'm amazed that he isn't trying to <u>break</u> that glass--but he never does

-1:05:42 "Quick, rewind it!"   A rewind function on a magic mirror?

-1:05:50 Sure is lucky the forest friends saw Shrek's capture!

-1:08:20 Pinocchio is a wooden boy--why would he have any underwear on, much less women's?

-1:12:51 Mongo the great stomps towards the castle.   Where in the world did the Muffin Man get gumdrops the size of Walla Walla?

-1:14:18 Shrek sure is tough, swinging down the chain like that and not hurting his hands

-1:16:40 If Fiona doesn't want Charming to kiss her, she sure waits a long ten seconds before hitting him

-1:17:54 Nice of Harold's crown to downsize to fit his froggy self

-1:19:33 They have until the twelfth stroke of midnight to make up their minds.   This ain't the only movie to pull this one: "On the stroke of midnight" this or that special thing happens.   Midnight, dear readers, is marked by the moment when the clock reaches 12:00:00.   Not on the twelfth stroke of the bell, which is generally around 12:00:44. Why does everybody get that extra forty-five seconds?

-1:19:44 Why does the "final moment" of the spell lift Shrek and Donkey into the air like that?

-1:20:04 Something to be thankful for: the potion's initial change left cute, button-nose Shrek in his old ogre clothing.   Fortunately for all of us, the return to normal put his old clothes back on, and didn't leave him in his knightly garb--which would have ripped asunder, leaving him starkers

-1:20:15 Why did the spell reversal lower Shrek gently to the ground, and drop Donkey on his ass?   (ha ha)

-1:21:22 What cat, anywhere, in the history of ever, has <u>voluntarily</u> gotten wet?   Puss really gets into his stage performances!

-1:21:30 He really gets dry fast, too

-1:21:35 Seems odd for the Forest Friends to bring the Magic Mirror with them--especially since apparently Dragon flew them in (otherwise how'd they get on-scene so fast to help Shrek?   The two ogres were in a carriage for, like, days to get to Far Far Away)

-1:24:48 I haven't given the Will Award out yet. Was saving it for...right now!   Donkey...and Dragon...have <u>children</u>?   How in the medieval world did <u>those</u> physics work out?

#19: Harry Potter and the Chamber of Secrets

Ruminations: this nitpicking Volume sure has a high concentration of Harry Potter films.   Last one, though.

-0:03:17Mr. Dursley has made it clear any noise and Harry is throttled.   Now Dobby the Extremely Annoying House Elf is banging his head against the dresser, and Harry stands there with the door open?

-0:04:15Dobby is a very, VERY well-done effect.   But right here as he hits his head there are continuity errors

-0:09:15No glass in Harry's bedroom window? They live in England, not the tropics—that must get very cold

-0:09:48 Continuity as Harry escapes out the window

-0:09:58   Continuity as Dursley falls out the window

-0:10:00The rope tied from the car to the window should still be attached to the car, but has disappeared...

-0:10:04Dursley falls straight out the window into the bushes below.   Shouldn't he be landing on the bars and such that were just yanked off the building?   They're down here somewhere!

-0:11:03   Magic dishes really, really well done

-0:11:29   Magic knitting is also really well done, but one wonders: with the magic knitting and magic dishes and all...what <u>does</u> Mrs. Weasley do all day?

-0:14:00Looking at the book list "There's only one place we're going to get all this—Diagon Alley!"   Well, <u>duh</u>

-0:15:15Nice of the floo powder mistake to allow Harry to pick up a plot point or two, no?

-0:15:52Harry taps on a glass jar of skulls.   Why? Expecting them to burst into song?

-0:16:10Mr. Potter's entrance was rather loud— nobody comes to check?   He's able to just walk out of the shop which is unlocked?   In this part of town, I wouldn't expect such a lack of security, especially since that fireplace allows anybody with floo powder to waltz right in. Which makes one wonder how magical locations handle security?   Bars across the fireplace?   Magic "No Floo Entrance" spells?   (Why didn't this nasty Knockturn Alley shop have such?)

-0:17:45Harry got lost in Knockturn Alley on the way to Diagon Alley.   He should've known it was a bad part of town, Knockturn Alley being right off Aton Alley, Crimin Alley, Infern Alley and Termin Alley...

-0:17:50As a lifelong four-eyes, I am <u>so</u> jealous of "ocular reparo."   One wonders if there isn't a magical spell to fix vision, though.   Maybe a shop on Medicin Alley?

-0:17:55 Boy, everybody sure hit puberty during the summer!   Compare this film to the first one...Ron, Harry, Hermione and even Malfoy were sure eating their magical Wheaties!   (Lucky Charms?)

-0:18:00 Lockhart's "Magical Me" book cover comes complete with thunder sound-effects?

-0:19:29 The Daily Prophet photographer takes a shot of happy Lockhart and reluctant Harry.   So...in the paper tomorrow, what will the moving shot show?   Harry edging away?

-0:22:10 Lucius Malfoy messes with the Weasleys in the shop corridor for three minutes—nobody needed to get past in that time?

-0:22:40 Trouble on Platform 9 ¾!   Convenient that mom and dad went through before Harry and Ron tried, leaving them alone when they fail.   And funny how nobody seems to worry about Muggles noticing what they're doing

-0:24:24 The flying car takes off and Ron points it skyward—how does one tell a flying car to go up or down?   I mean, left and right make sense but...

-0:24:47 When the boys first find the railroad tracks to follow to Hogwarts, there's no train in sight.   Fifteen seconds later they're almost run over...how fast is this train moving?

-0:25:00 Harry's in a flying car, and he didn't think to lock the door and put his seatbelt on?? How can he be falling out at this point?

-0:26:40 The Whomping Willow has been at Hogwarts since "before you both were born" (Harry and Ron). So...how come we didn't catch sight of it last year?

-0:27:30 continuity, windshield breakage

-0:27:41 The car falls out of the tree awfully slowly

-0:27:48 There's a light here on Harry and Ron's faces—from where?

-0:28:08 How does this flying car eject its occupants? For that matter, how does a "simple" flying enchantment confer sentience?

-0:29:32 The boys took off in the middle of a London day, and only 7 muggles saw the flying car??

-0:29:33 Snape holds a Daily Prophet with a pic of the boys and the flying car zooming right at the lens. So...who took the midair picture? Complete with sound?

-0:30:00 Why is Snape reading the riot act, and not McGonagle? Oh, wait—here she comes

-0:31:30 I believe this is the first time we see Professor Sprout—where was she last year?

-0:32:00 How convenient that the children are working with mandrakes, when Hogwarts students are soon to be petrified!!

-0:35:00 Howler <u>very</u> well done

-0:37:27 Does it make sense that the Lockhart in the picture is running away from the roomful of pixies?

-0:37:52 Hermione shouts "Immobulus" and the pixies freeze.   Well, almost—they can still blink.   Plus Neville doesn't freeze—why?

-0:39:20 Ron pulls out his wand to hex Draco, and throws a hex (which backfires) without any words.   Usually spells require sound, don't they?   It's also odd that Draco does nothing to defend himself

-0:40:00 I really, really could have done without the slug-burping

-0:40:26 Knowing that Draco said "mudblood", I am surprised Hagrid does nothing—the boy needs detention at the very least!

-0:44:12 PVP—there are huge bloody letters on the wall, and nobody has noticed them for thirty seconds

-0:44:18 "It's written in blood."   How can they tell? It must not smell like blood, or they would've noticed earlier. And whose blood is it?   Mrs. Norris is just petrified, she's not dead.   Turns out later that Ginny Weasley (under Tom Riddle's spell) made this happen…how in the world did 5 foot Ginny write those letters at a 7 foot height?

-0:44:55 "You'll be next, mudbloods."   How does Draco keep avoiding punishment?

-0:47:45 The Hogwarts staircases are often in motion and loud about it.   Except when somebody is trying to get dialogue out—nice of them

-0:48:37 Creepy, if you think about it…"We will be transforming animals" well, birds, but anyway "into water goblets."   Doesn't this hurt the animal or bird in question? And why does Ron not tell somebody about his wand problem?   And when he turns Scabbers almost into a goblet, why is there just a twitching tail and not further movement— assuming the rat is still conscious and aware of his ghastly current fate?

-0:50:08 Every witch or wizard who has "gone bad" has come from Slytherin House.   So why does this house still exist?   Disband, already!

-0:52:20 I used to be in school (I swear) and Hogwarts sure works differently than any school I've heard about—Hermione walks up to Ron and Harry in the hallway, students all around, says "Here's the polyjuice potion."   Like nobody was listening in, or would say anything about the potion they're not supposed to have?

-0:52:27 It's going to take a month to make this potion.   Hogwarts is in trouble—isn't there an invisibility cloak plan we can try?

-0:53:45 See Sorcerer's Stone nitpicking...but once again, how does the Quaffle get back in play, after thrown through the hoop, and why does the point marker have three numeral entry, when every Quidditch score is worth xx0 points?   (10, 50, 150, etc)

-0:55:15 Turns out one of the Bludgers has gone rogue.   Why isn't the game immediately halted?   Harry is in danger for over two minutes—and then arm is broken anyway!

-1:02:35 Colin Creevy is petrified, in the hospital wing.   They took him all the way there without pulling the camera out of his hands?   And if he was petrified while taking a picture, why is his camera eye closed?

-1:02:45 Either this is a magical camera, or Dumbledore don't know nothin' bout takin' no pictures.   He just opens the back of a film camera—which would normally mean the exposed film would be ruined.   (This I know from long experience.)   However, this particular film explodes? Was it, too, frightened by the basilisk?

-1:03:00 Gee, this seems like it would be a good time for Harry to <u>tell Dumbledore about the voice he's been hearing</u>...but no

-1:03:35 "Why are we in the girls' lavatory?"   He's just <u>now</u> asking this?   They've been in there quite a while...

-1:06:24 Dueling time, and out of the hundred or so students in the room, it ends up being Potter v. Malfoy? What are the odds?

-1:07:30 What <u>does</u> Malfoy have to do to get in trouble at Hogwarts?   Now he's cheating during the dangerous duel, and no detention, no reprimand...

-1:07:56 Now Malfoy has created a very dangerous, could-bite-anybody-<u>snake</u> and nothing is being done to stop him

-1:10:30 1,000 years later Slytherin only has <u>one</u> heir?   Extremely unlikely

-1:12:01 Of course Harry, and nobody else, discovers third attack.   And how is a <u>ghost</u> petrified?   How do you petrify something already dead?

-1:16:53 Hey, Harry's all alone with Dumbledore, in the safety of his office!   Maybe <u>now</u> he'll talk about that strange voice he's hearing...never mind

-1:15:07 What are the odds Harry would get to Dumbledore's office <u>just</u> as Fawkes goes nova?

-1:16:10 Lucky somebody told Harry about phoenixes, seeing as how he'll need that info later

-1:18:42 Why is Ron still carrying his broken, dangerous-to-him and basically useless wand around?

-1:19:10 Magicked cupcakes left for Crabbe and Goyle.   Mmm...air cake!   I know if I was going to a magical school and I saw a cupcake <u>hanging in midair</u>, I would definitely just snork it right down

-1:19:28 Since the cupcakes make the boys fall immediately asleep, sure is lucky for them they don't choke, or hit their heads on the stone floor

-1:20:44 I would imagine the polyjuice changeover experience would be <u>very</u> painful, but Harry doesn't seem to mind

-1:20:52 Why doesn't he immediately take his glasses off, once turned into Crabbe?   Does Crabbe have an undiagnosed myopia?

-1:21:04 The potion changes the taker into the intended person...why does it just work on the outside? Shouldn't a person's voice change as well?   Harry is quite a bit shorter than Crabbe—do his insides not match up as well?

If they do...why are his vocal cords unchanged?   Huh?
Huh?

-1:21:31 Crabbe/Harry <u>still</u> has his glasses on!!
Why?

-1:23:07 Seems odd that Malfoy is the only one in
the common room

-1:24:42 So the polyjuice potion works for an hour.
Once you take it, you have sixty minutes, give-or-take, until
you revert.   Crabbe/Harry and Goyle/Ron have been sitting
with Malfoy for about three minutes, and suddenly the
potion is wearing off.

So...what were they doing for the <u>fifty-seven</u>
minutes it took them to get to the Slytherin common room?

-1:25:00 Maybe he just got used to not having
them—Harry is himself again...and now he's <u>not</u> wearing his
glasses

-1:27:10 Of course Harry, and nobody else in this
busy castle, discovers the discarded diary

-1:27:36 Tom Marvolo Riddle equaling I Am Lord
Voldemort is absolutely <u>brilliant</u>

-1:28:06 Harry puts a dab of ink onto the diary page,
which disappears.   Why would he bother writing anything
else?

-1:28:13 The words Harry writes don't disappear the way the inkblot did.   Why?

-1:28:30 Harry has a book in his possession that writes back, that he knows nothing else about—and the <u>first</u> thing he asks is Chamber of Secrets related.   This kid is <u>very</u> focused!

-1:29:30 ...and how, exactly, does this diary <u>suck</u> Harry into its pages?

-1:31:40 Harry is intangible, in a Scrooge-on-his-three-spirits-quest kinda way.   I have the same problem here as I do with Scrooge...how does our boy hear?   See? Not pass through the floor when he can pass through everything else?   Chalk it up to magic, I guess...

-1:31:45 The effect is very well done—that only Harry has any color

-1:33:04 How does the diary know that Harry has seen what he needs to, and it's time to send him back?

-1:33:30 Harry returns to his room and its night—he proceeds to rush off out of shot.   Next frame it's morning, and Harry is just telling Ron and Hermione about his discovery.   What did he rush off for?   (Ah—bathroom break)

-1:35:00 Harry discovers a burglar has been through his room.   We later learn this was Ginny, looking for the diary.   What was the point of going through his room like a dervish—and how'd she get in, anyway?   Since when can girls get into boy dormitories?

-1:38:47 invisibility cloak effect <u>so good</u>!!

-1:39:40 Hagrid said he was expecting Harry and company.   So why answer the door with a loaded crossbow?

-1:40:03 Lucky it's possible to see through this cloak of invisibility

-1:40:50 "You mark my words, there'll be killings next."   Makes it sound like the bad guy has been holding back—when it's only sheer dumb <u>luck</u> that nobody is dead yet!

-1:41:48 Why is Dumbledore the only one who can see the cloaked figures?

-1:42:30 Every time somebody notices the marching spiders, there's bunches of them to see.   But nobody seems to be shrieking or looking around for spiders <u>except</u> when we need to see them.   There's an infestation in and around the castle—but everybody's pretty blasé about it!

-1:42:40 It's important to <u>not</u> be caught outside the castle at night, but the boys leave the invisibility cloak behind

(?) and sneak out of Hagrid's very shortly after the others leave, probably soon enough that they could be caught

-1:43:23 Hagrid is taken away...why are the lights left on in his place?   Why is there an untended fire left blazing out front?   Seems like they would give him a moment to "lock up," as it were

-1:43:30 And why do the boys take Fang with them into the forest?   If they were paying attention last year, they know he's a useless coward

-1:44:27 "Follow the spiders."   And they are, and there are tons of the little buggers all around—seems like we should be hearing squishing sounds but (thankfully) Harry and Ron seem to know just where to step

-1:45:45 I really, really could have done without the giant spider scenes

-1:46:03 Convenient for the story, but why does Aragog have the power of speech?   (And know English?)

-1:46:33 Why, exactly, are the spiders terrified of the basilisk?

-1:47:54 WILL AWARD alert!   For inexcusable implausibility, the WA goes to the timely Flying Car Rescue! What severe luck our heroes must have that this poor magicked Ford Anglia has become sentient, and yet not too feral to notice former masters and come to their rescue!!   (It would be a delicate balance, I'm sure!!)

-1:49:09 Not that I'm complaining, but what keeps the giant spiders in the forest, and out of Hogwarts?   (There sure are enough of the small ones, is all I'm sayin')

-1:49:15 The car showed up to help all by itself—why is it now necessary for Ron to drive?

-1:49:48 "The flying gear's jammed?"   So...the magical flying car has a gear to accomplish the flying? (Maybe it's not magical so much as futuristic!)

-1:51:35 Hermione has been in hospital for how long—and they only now discover she's got parchment in her hand?

-1:55:10 The monster has "taken" Ginny into the Chamber.   Which is a good trick, considering snakes (even giant ones) don't have hands.   Apparently the basilisk swallowed her for travel?

-2:00:17 Down into the pipes they go—how come Lockhart fell for about three seconds, yet Harry and Ron slide for ages?

-2:02:10 Lucky the cave-in just missed Harry, huh?

-2:04:55 Harry's specific instructions: "<u>Any</u> sign of movement, close your eyes." So it's surprising that when Tom Riddle walks in, Harry looks right at him

-2:05:58 Ginny wrote the messages on the wall? I've been over this already, but it bears repeating: with whose blood (everybody was just petrified) and with what <u>stepladder</u>?

-2:08:05 Good thing for the drama that Riddle went with Lord Voldemort, and not Lord Tromdelov or Lord Dorvelomt

-2:08:49 Sure is lucky that Harry gets a chance to be loyal to Dumbledore, and said loyalty draws Fawkes to him...seeing as how our boy had <u>no</u> plan whatsoever

-2:09:25 Riddle uses parseltongue to summon the basilisk. I suppose the snake might not want to obey any other master, but Harry could at least <u>try</u> saying "Go away", since he speaks parseltongue

-2:12:50 Wow, that Gryffindor sword is lame. Looks like a dollar store toy

-2:13:10 What was the point of Harry climbing the statue?

-2:13:34 Lucky Riddle just watches Harry fight his monster—no "Expelliarmus" or "Alohamora" or anything

-2:15:23 Seems like a huge leap in logic for Harry to decide upon stabbing the fang into the book

-2:16:15 Wow, Ginny has recuperative powers! She's just about all better right here, where thirty seconds ago she was "mostly dead."

-2:16:40 Harry, to Ginny: "You need to get yourself out."   And how will she or Ron manage that long, smooth climb?

-2:17:10 Since when do birds have tear ducts?

-2:17:30 Wow, Harry has recuperative powers!   He seems all better, when thirty seconds ago he was "mostly dead"

-2:19:20 So now Harry tells Dumbledore about being a parseltongue.   After it's far too late to be of any use

-2:20:54 Harry and Dumbledore look at the Sword of Gryffindor, this incredibly important artifact...that nobody has cleaned the basilisk blood off of?

-2:22:49 Weird light on Lucius Malfoy's face right here

-2:22:55 That one fang strike made a hole straight through the book?   Seems surprising

-2:24:10 I'm not sure why Dumbledore just gives the diary to Harry

-2:25:00 "Give a house elf clothes, you set that house elf free."   The definition of "clothes" seems <u>really</u> flimsy.   One sock=clothes, and it doesn't even have to belong to the owner?   People must lose house elves all the time

-2:28:17 To celebrate the unpetrifications and destruction of the monster, all exams are cancelled?   Some place of learning <u>this</u> is!

-2:28:40 Huh.   Hagrid sure looks good for just having gotten out of Azkaban—I heard that place was tough. And Ron sent <u>Errol</u> to spring him?   Couldn't they have used a less reliable means of communication?

#20: Finding Nemo

<u>Ruminations:</u>   Something about the vast, open ocean enables the filmmakers to consistently freak me out. I know the moment the barracuda will show up, I know when the big diver is going to slide in, I know when the sharks will suddenly appear--and the last few times I've seen the film it's been on a home screen, not even at the theater...but all that open water still gives me the creeps!   I jump <u>every</u> time!

I also understand that there are so many volumetric water effects, so much attention to detail that every frame of the water sequences in this movie took up to <u>four days</u> to render.   Which is probably why the water looks so real...

One last thing: no timecode for you.   Sorry, Gremlins got to the word-processing program.   (That's what I get for feeding them in the shower after midnight)

-This nit is one of those things that is absolutely necessary for the purposes of the story the filmmakers are trying to tell, but...as a human being who can pretty much only converse in English, there are billions of fellow human beings in this world that I would have a very hard time communicating with.   In Finding Nemo, however, clownfish talk to whales talk to turtles talk to pelicans talk to sharks talk to starfish talk to crabs talk to seagulls...

-Marlin is so excited about he and Coral's new home. Why is the drop-off such a wonderful fish home location?   It appears to be a very high-crime sort of neighborhood.

-"In a couple of days we're going to be parents!"   The eggs are already laid...aren't they parents already?

-Coral likes the name Nemo.   Is she a Latin scholar? A big reader?   Fan of Disney movies?   Where does her name choice come from?

-After the barracuda strike, when Marlin wakes up and goes to check on his children, the nursery is blacked out as he approaches...yet as he looks inside, it's lit.

-Marlin can see tadpole Nemo moving around in his sac.   How, unless the sac is lit from inside?

-Why does a cracked egg sac correspond to a gimpy fin?

-The other fish that were all cavorting in this neighborhood have disappeared.   Do they have some sort of barracuda radar that Marlin & Coral do not?

-After Marlin hits the barracuda, the 'cuda changes position when the shot changes.

-Would a barracuda even <u>notice</u> the strike of a clownfish, much less be moved by it?

-Are barracudas big caviar eaters?   Why did it trash almost all of the eggs?

-So...fish sleep?   On their sides, just like a human? (I did not know that!)

-Nemo is so excited about going to school that he slips out of the nest--just barely, it seems like.   Next shot, though, he's <u>buried</u> nose first in a sea-plant.   He just edged out of the nest, how did he get so stuck?

-"Forget to brush?"   What, exactly, do fish have to brush?   (And how do they brush it?)

-Okay, fish swim in schools, and it's clever that Nemo's class really is a "school."   However, I was under the impression that fish swam in schools of similar fish.   (Forced bussing, maybe?)

-Did Marlin not tell his son where Mommy and all eight zillion of his brothers and sisters went?   It seems odd that Nemo would <u>want</u> to see a shark, considering the truly horrible circumstances of his birth...

-One of Nemo's new friends is "H2O intolerant". It must be a <u>very</u> mild case, since he's breathing nothing but water yet only sneezes twice.

-Buckteeth? On a <u>fish</u>? (Okay, I can see what <u>he</u> needs to brush.)

-If the barracuda had not attacked, Nemo would now be one of several hundred young clownfish. Yet at school, there doesn't seem to be more than a half-dozen of any other family. Do clownfish produce many more eggs than most fish, or did the barracuda ravage all these families? (I know, I'm a sick man. Let's move on...)

-It's just a joke on the filmmakers' part, the "stoplight" with the fish...but I will question one thing: why do the fish swim in lanes, anyway? They have the whole ocean!

-Marlin finds out the school is going to the drop-off and overreacts. "Why don't they just fry 'em up now, and serve 'em with chips?" How does he know we humans do that to fish? He get up to the mainland a lot?

-PVP: Nemo and Marlin are having a tiff, and suddenly an enormous diver comes up behind Nemo. <u>Neither</u> knew he was coming? The fish back at the drop-off all seem surprised, also.

-I can only imagine the school newsletter. "New Kid Disappears at Drop-Off!"

-Nemo shrieks even out of the water as the diver is fish-napping him.   How does he draw breath to scream with out of water?   His father shouts his name a moment later, again above water--how?

-The strange diver captures Nemo and heads back to the 'butt'.   He climbs in, the second diver climbs in and three seconds later the engine starts up.   Somebody is sure in a hurry!

-Considering the rush his friend is in, it's kinda stupid that the diver would put his goggles on the boat's railing.

-Dori has a short-term memory problem.   (A very funny plot device.)   She says "It runs in my family...at least I think it does."   A funny line, but whether or not her family has a history of short-term memory loss should be a long-term memory for her.

-Both the barracuda and the shark teeth-snapping sounds are metallic.   Neither creature has metal teeth, though.

-PVP: the two fishies are completely unaware that a shark the size of New Hampshire is right there?

-Dori is really laid-back about attending the shark's FA meeting (Fish-eaters Anonymous.)   Does her long-term memory not have any warnings about sharks in it?

-"Hey, look!   Balloons!"   "Those aren't balloons." How does he know?

-Speaking of FA, the motto is "Fish are friends, not food." So...what exactly are the sharks going to eat? Kelp?

-Runner-up for the <u>Will Award</u>: the absolutely necessary goggles, that could have fallen anywhere along the boat's journey, just happen to fall right where Dori and Marlin will come across them while being chased by Bruce. Pretty lucky...

-You know the shark is called Bruce after the movie <u>Jaws</u>, as that was the name of the mechanical shark in that movie, right? Okay. Moving on. Compared with our first view of Bruce (the one where I almost soiled myself, in the theater), it sure seems like he gets smaller in order to fit through the submarine's passageways.

-"Heeeere's Brucie!" How has a shark seen <u>The Shining</u>?

-Bruce's FA friends show up all of a sudden to stop him, when they were nowhere in sight a moment before.

-The goggles coming to rest at the submarine pretty much means the boat went <u>right over</u> the depth-charge area. Does that seem right?

-Apparently all of the crewmembers of the drowned submarine got off safely, and a good thing, too: running across a couple of dead humans would sure have changed the tone of this kid's movie, wouldn't it?

-The depth charges all go off and yet only <u>one</u> bubble reaches the surface?   (It makes for a funny joke, but I'm not buying)

-It seems strange that as Nemo is put into the fish tank, all the other fish are nowhere to be seen, even the starfish.   Is there a reason--well, besides Darla--why they all would hide?

-I'll buy that the fish know what store they were bought in, but the <u>starfish</u> has a comprehension of <u>Ebay</u>? Naw...

-Jacques cleans Nemo.   What exactly does he do, and why does Nemo <u>glow</u> afterwards?

-Blowfish can't just blow up and deflate at a moment's notice.   Sorry, kids, it doesn't work like that. Furthermore, the first time the blowfish deflates, off-screen, all of the plants in the tank move as if a wind is blowing. <u>Wind</u> in a fish tank?

-Gil tells Peach the starfish that they can't hear her. She pulls away, says something, and reattaches...and continues talking.   Didn't he just say they can't hear her when she's like that?   (Except somehow this time they can.)

-When Nigel the pelican comes in, he can hear what Peach is saying, though she's attached to the inside of the fish tank...and what kind of dentist can ignore a pelican on the windowsill for minutes on end?

-P. Sherman (42 Wallaby Way, Sydney) feels proud that he saved Nemo from dying out in the wide open ocean...but has no problems giving the fish to Darla.   (Classic case of denial.)

-Note: "The sea monkey has my money."   This is one of the non sequiturs Dori tosses out while Marlin is trying to wake her up...and in my opinion might be the funniest movie line <u>ever</u>.   Not just in an animated film, <u>ever</u>!

-Dori needs the light from the deep-dweller to read the P. Sherman diving mask.   The light-providing fish is chasing Marlin hither and yon, yet the light on the mask stays steady for a remarkably long time.   Then once the fish gets stuck, it sits around and waits patiently while Marlin & Dori discuss what to do.

-As Dori and Marlin search for the mask, escape the submarine, and deal with the deep-dwelling fish, Dori seems to retain her knowledge of the situation.   We're to believe that somehow Marlin coming into Dori's life helps her with her memory problem.   Why?

-"All drains lead to the ocean."   Well, yes...but put a water-processing plant between the two, and Nemo is <u>not</u> going to get to the ocean in one piece.

-At the start of the "Nemo joining the club" scene, we again see him <u>sleeping</u> on his side.

-Did the other fish pull Peach off the side of the tank and stick her to the volcano?   And how does the blowfish get his voice to echo like that?

-When Jacques turns on the Ring of Fire, there's a squeaky sound-effect.   No such effect, though, when he turns it <u>off</u>.

-At the line "We can't send him off to his death" (Ring of Fire scene), Nemo changes positions as the shot changes.

-Look for the <u>Toy Story</u> "YO" truck driving by during Gil's escape fantasy.

-The silver-colored fish collective: the shape-making is fun, I love it--but how do they move together as one when not connected?   Furthermore, when they make the arrow shape, how do they light on-and-off?

-PVP when Dori and Marlin encounter the jellyfish. Dori's playing with her new little toy; "And you shall be my Squishee."   They don't see an entire sea's worth of jellyfish all around?

-Everything in the ocean talks--why are the deep-dweller and the jellyfish silent?

-In the downward-looking shot during the jellyfish bouncing, the trench the two were supposed to go through has disappeared.

-Only Nemo is small enough to get into the filter, so how does Gill even know what to describe in there?   How could he have seen it?

-Crush doesn't want Marlin to hurl on his shell as it's freshly waxed.   Why would a turtle wax his shell, and where would he get the wax from?

-Does a real current have roller-coaster-like sections?

-"She's sub-level, dude."   Marlin swims down to where Dori is resting on a turtle, and two turtles part to show him where she is.   Next shot, these parting turtles have disappeared.

-When Nemo reacts to Squirt flying out of the current, suddenly Crush is right next to him out of nowhere.

-Little turtle Squirt tumbles out of the East Australian Current into the open sea, and is out for some time.   The current is moving along without him, yet when he pushes back in, he's not that far behind everybody else.

-All of Australia is talking about Marlin's search for Nemo, including a dolphin that tells each next bit of his story every time he pops out of the water.   The dolphin is a fish--if he can only talk in one place, I would think it would be in the water, not out of it.

-Beyond the fact that swordfish are, um, swordfighting, why do their "swords" make metallic noises?

-"In forty-eight hours this tank will be filthy."   How does Gil know this?   Does he do this sort of thing a lot?

-Just as every window in France looks out on the Eiffel tower, and every window in Manhattan has a view of the Empire State building, so does every spot in Sydney harbor offer a view of the famous opera house.

-Why does the new, fancy filter talk?   For the benefit of the fish?

-As previously mentioned, birds talk to fish talk to mammals...why do the seagulls only say "mine?"

-When the pelican hears about Marlin, he drops the crab he was about to snack on.   The seagulls approach the crab, who waves chop-socky claws at them.   Yet he was seemingly content to be pelican food a moment before.

-When Nigel the pelican slams into the dentist's window, his face is pointed to the right, but next frame it's smashed against the window to the left.   His hit also knocks the frame out of the window, yet next shot it's fixed.

-Favorite freeze-frame moment of Finding Nemo: in this same moment when the pelican smacks the window, wait until the shot gets to the dentist, and stop the DVD. What do you know?   The tooth is already out of the guy's mouth--before the dentist jerks back!   He already got the tooth out before the pelican hit--so what is the guy complaining about?

-PVP: Nigel smacks the window and then hides just below.   The dentist opens this same window and looks out...and <u>doesn't</u> see a pelican a foot below him, hiding?

-Yet again Nigel can understand Peach even though she's on the other side of the glass.

-Nigel goes into a long explanation for Nemo about what is going on with his dad.   Have the dentist and his patient left the room?

-On his second try, Nemo goes through the filter wheel upright, which he shouldn't be able to do.

-A <u>burping</u> fish?   Really?

-P. Sherman (42 Wallaby Way, Sydney) puts a hand into the tank to check the filthiness quotient, then pulls his arm out again--and his arm is completely dry.

-Dori: "What is it with men and asking for directions?"   I dunno, but since Marlin is a <u>fish</u>, I'm not sure her question applies to the situation anyway.

-Gee, sure is <u>bright</u> inside the whale.   One wonders where the light source is coming from...

-Do whales really have uvulas?   Taste buds?   Giant human-like tongues?   Well, one thing I know they don't have, and that's any sort of connecting passageway between their mouths and their blowholes.   Dori and Marlin <u>couldn't</u> be expelled that way.

-How does Marlin know about Moby Dick?   (That well-read wife of his?)

-Dori and Marlin, inside the whale, speak and shout while out of water without any apparent breathing problems.

-All the fish in the tank seem so surprised when the net scoops up Nemo.   Nobody felt the oncoming pressure wave of a hand in the tank?   Nobody saw the dentist coming?

-More out of water talking during the Darla scene.

-Nigel saves Marlin and Dori from his fellow pelican, and the two fish flop down the length of the pier.   Um...why don't they flop themselves back into the water?

-As Nigel tries to convince Marlin and Dori that he's a friend, suddenly seagulls appear out of nowhere--including in the direction we were already looking.

-Nigel: "Don't make any sudden moves, but hop in my mouth."   He needs to make up his mind--are they hopping, or are they not making any sudden moves?

-Those are some sharp seagull beaks to go right through a sail like that.

-It's interesting--and a little creepy--that Nigel goes about saving Nemo, when some other, less-important fish was probably breakfast.

-If the dentist really hit himself on the light hard enough to knock himself out, that light should've moved more.

-In the dentist office confusion, Darla pulls on the dentist's sink, and breaks it.   (Seriously poor workmanship!) Then water shoots out of the bowl and hits her in the face. Does that seem right?

-As all of the chaos is going on in the dentist's office, the receptionist and the guy reading the paper are just sitting there, doing nothing.   Does that seem right?

-The crabs around the water pipe's exit make a big deal about staying away from their pipe, "This is our spot", yet the next seven pipe exits are unmanned.   What's so special about the one they're on?

-The Will Award: Nemo pops out of the pipe, having just missed catching his father on the way by, but swims right to where Dori (whom he doesn't know) is circling.   A few degrees off and he would have missed her entirely.

-Nemo meets Dori and Dori suddenly remembers everything.   If you freeze-frame through the montage of her remembering, there's a shot of her unconscious on the goggles, and unconscious on a jellyfish.   How would she remember things that happened while she was knocked out?

-Dori and Nemo start calling out to Marlin.   Is he so zoned out that he can't hear them?   Sound travels <u>really</u> well underwater--it's not like he's too far away...

-The crab doesn't want to tell Dori which way Marlin went, so she drags him all the way to the surface, threatening him with seagulls, so he'll talk.   Are his claws ornamental? She got him all the way to the surface with no trouble?

-Marlin tries to convince Nemo not to swim into the net to save Dori.   Nemo says "There's no time!" to his dad, yet spends another eight seconds having a 'moment' with him.

-I can't think of a way to prove it, but the "swim down" physics don't seem like they would work.

-Apparently the trawler's crew is incredibly surprised by the fish working together.   So surprised, that they allow the whole yardarm to break, losing it and the net, rather than releasing the net and letting the fish go.   Pretty dumb, if you think about it.

-It's also surprising that a net full of fish could pull the whole boat to one side, and that the torque required to pull the boat like that wouldn't snap the spar a <u>lot</u> sooner.

-The down-swimming fish break the trawler's spar-- yet the broken piece and the bell never do show as the net falls to the ocean floor.

-The FA sharks go so far as to visit the little fish school?   Sure, <u>we</u> know they don't eat fish anymore, but wouldn't this be worrisome to some of the fish that don't?

-All the fish escaping in the baggies is ever-so-slightly improbable.   How do they get onto the windowsill?   How do they get to the ground without the bags breaking?   Up onto the curb?   Why would a car honk at a starfish?

-P. Sherman's fish are all bobbing around in their little baggies at the end--the water level in the bags should match the ocean's water level, therefore making the bags much lower in the water.

Afterword

Thanks for playing--and keep up looking for nits! If you just couldn't get enough, www.slipups.com has more, as well as Volumes 1 and 3-5 of this very series.

But I gotta go back to the movies...

Printed in Poland
by Amazon Fulfillment
Poland Sp. z o.o., Wrocław